# Cambridge Elements ≡

Elements in International Relations
edited by
Jon C. W. Pevehouse
*University of Wisconsin–Madison*
Tanja A. Börzel
*Freie Universität Berlin*
Edward D. Mansfield
*University of Pennsylvania*

# THE DUAL NATURE OF MULTILATERAL DEVELOPMENT BANKS

## *Balancing Development and Financial Logics*

Laura Francesca Peitz
*The Hertie School, Berlin*

CAMBRIDGE
UNIVERSITY PRESS

Shaftesbury Road, Cambridge CB2 8EA, United Kingdom

One Liberty Plaza, 20th Floor, New York, NY 10006, USA

477 Williamstown Road, Port Melbourne, VIC 3207, Australia

314–321, 3rd Floor, Plot 3, Splendor Forum, Jasola District Centre,
New Delhi – 110025, India

103 Penang Road, #05–06/07, Visioncrest Commercial, Singapore 238467

Cambridge University Press is part of Cambridge University Press & Assessment,
a department of the University of Cambridge.

We share the University's mission to contribute to society through the pursuit of
education, learning and research at the highest international levels of excellence.

www.cambridge.org
Information on this title: www.cambridge.org/9781009392303

DOI: 10.1017/9781009392297

First published 2023

A catalogue record for this publication is available from the British Library.

ISBN 978-1-009-39230-3 Paperback
ISSN 2515-706X (online)
ISSN 2515-7302 (print)

# The Dual Nature of Multilateral Development Banks

## Balancing Development and Financial Logics

Elements in International Relations

DOI: 10.1017/9781009392297
First published online: March 2023

Laura Francesca Peitz
*The Hertie School, Berlin*

Author for correspondence: Laura Francesca Peitz, laura.peitz@posteo.de

**Abstract:** This Element offers a novel, highly relevant perspective toward Multilateral Development Banks (MDBs), which are development and financial organizations at the same time. Based on the elaborate institutional logics perspective borrowed from organizational sociology, it uncovers the complex trade-offs between financial and development pressures faced by MDBs and explains variation in organizational responses thereto across types of MDBs. The argument is tested with an original dataset using Data Envelopment Analysis to explain variation in response patterns across MDBs. The analysis shows that private-sector lending as well as a shareholder majority of borrowing-members pull MDBs into the direction of the financial nature, at the expense of the development nature. Thereby, this Element provides unique insights into MDBs' responses to their dual nature and significantly advances the understanding of MDB lending operations, drawing attention to the complexities involved in the unique MDB business model.

**Keywords:** international organizations, global economic governance, development lending, institutional complexity, data envelopment analysis

ISBNs: 9781009392303 (PB), 9781009392297 (OC)
ISSNs: 2515-706X (online), 2515-7302 (print)

# Contents

# 1 Introduction: The Duality of MDBs

From financing the Sustainable Development Goals, through tackling fragility and violent conflict as well as responding to forced migration crises around the globe, to swiftly reacting to the COVID-19 pandemic, Multilateral Development Banks (MDBs) are relevant players in a wide range of global challenges and for this reason have noticeably (re)gained academic and policy attention in recent years. Their success (Birdsall and Morris, 2016, p. 1) is at least partly based on a business model that is unique among International Organizations (IOs): MDBs are simultaneously development and financial organizations. As development organizations, they serve a public policy purpose; as financial organizations, financed by bond issuance in private capital markets, MDBs need to ensure financial viability. This duality, which is inherent in every MDB, is the subject of this Element. I tackle the research questions of how the development and financial natures of MDBs are related and how distinct types of MDBs cope with their dual nature. Thereby, I draw academic attention to the relevance of MDBs' financial nature, and to the pressures resulting for their development operations – an aspect that despite its centrality has so far been largely neglected in MDB research. As a result, this Element contributes significantly to gaining a fuller understanding of the realities imposed by the unique business model of MDBs.

In this Element, I argue and empirically show that there is a trade-off between the two natures of MDBs, requiring a compromise between development and financial goals. My results show that MDBs settle with varying patterns of prioritization: some prioritize development over financial goals, while others show the inverse pattern of favoring conservative banking priorities at the cost of development-oriented lending. Based on this variance, MDBs can be located on a continuum spanning from commercial bank (clearly prioritizing the financial over the development nature) to aid agency (favoring the development over the financial nature). Interestingly, my key results reveal significantly different patterns of prioritization across distinct types of MDBs. First, and most importantly, prioritization varies with *portfolio structure*: MDBs lending to the public sector are more development oriented than MDBs lending primarily to private sector organizations. Second, MDB *shareholder structure* explains additional variation in prioritization. Keeping portfolio structure constant, MDBs owned primarily by borrowing member states are usually more oriented toward financial goals than MDBs where nonborrowing (sometimes falsely called donor) member states have a voting majority. This demonstrates the meaningfulness of a new MDB typology based on the two dimensions of portfolio and shareholder structures.

These results are based on innovative ways of conceptualizing and empirically analyzing the dual nature immanent in MDBs. To improve our understanding of the duality of MDBs and to hypothesize the organizational responses taken by them to cope with their duality, I import the institutional logics perspective (Thornton et al., 2015) from neo-institutional organization theory to the study of IOs. From this perspective, MDBs face two sets of competing demands, arising from two distinct institutional logics: promoting development in recipient countries, and maintaining the ability to raise resources in international capital markets at favorable rates. This duality results in a particularly challenging form of institutional complexity, the only viable strategic response to which is for MDBs to strike a compromise between the two logics. I illustrate how the two sets of demands manifest and conflict at diverse levels of MDBs' operations and explain where and how there is variation in MDB responses to the complexity they face. I derive two hypotheses, the first of them expecting a compromise that more strongly prioritizes development over financial demands at MDBs which lend primarily to the public compared to the private sector. The second hypothesis expects a stronger prioritization of development demands at MDBs that are owned predominantly by borrowing member states.

These hypotheses are tested in a comparative quantitative empirical analysis of MDB nonconcessional lending portfolio calibration. It is based on a novel dataset, originally assembled for this research, which covers a broad set of fifteen MDBs from 2010 to 2018. I employ Data Envelopment Analysis (DEA), a nonparametric frontier analysis method originating from organizational efficiency and performance analysis. This empirical approach allows me to systematically and comparatively assess the degree to which individual MDBs comply with development versus financial demands and thus the prioritization patterns put into practice by different (types of) MDBs to juggle their two conflicting natures.

In the remainder of this Element, I first briefly present the MDB business model and outline previous research as well as this Element's contribution to our understanding of MDBs. I then introduce the institutional logics perspective and apply it to the MDB context to derive two hypotheses. In Section 4, I describe the methodological approach taken as well as the dataset compiled for this research. Subsequently, I present my main findings, before discussing them in more depth and contextualizing them with knowledge gained through expert interviews in Section 6. The last section concludes.

## 2 Understanding MDBs

### 2.1 The MDB Business Model

MDBs are multilateral development finance organizations and defined here as organizations that are established via international treaties and are (primarily) owned by three or more sovereign states, are mandated with national (socio) economic development, and engage in bank-like transactions, primarily in the form of long-term lending, and of borrowing from financial markets (Peitz, 2022). This definition is at the same time more comprehensive and more rigorous than existing definitions, many of which tend to be too exclusive, nonsystematic, or ambiguous (cf. e.g. Bhargava, 2012; Braaten, 2014; Faure et al., 2015; Institute of Development Studies, 2000). It thus provides clear criteria for the inclusion even of less known, smaller MDBs, which are usually not systematically regarded or disregarded as MDBs. Overall, this definition currently pertains to a total of twenty-six MDBs (see Table A.1 in the Appendix for a complete list).

MDBs have a unique, powerful, and attractive financial model that clearly distinguishes them from other development agencies and IOs (for details, see Peitz, 2022). Just as the term Multilateral Development *Bank* suggests, these IOs are and operate like financial organizations, as is shown in Figure 1. MDBs are capitalized by their shareholders, who provide MDBs with capital proportional to the shares they hold, which forms (part of) MDBs' equity. Against this capital base, MDBs issue bonds and debt in private capital markets, that is, borrow from private investors. The resources thereby raised are then on-lent to MDB borrowers, which can be sovereign states and private sector entities. These, in turn, make principal payments on the loans received as well as pay interest rates and (potentially) fees. Net income generated from the payment of interest and fees can be allocated to reserves, which together with the paid-in capital provided by shareholders form MDBs' equity.

Central to the business model of MDBs is that they leverage their capital base, meaning that the amounts borrowed from capital markets exceed their equity. Hence, for every dollar in equity (which consists partly of shareholder contributions, partly of reserves) MDBs can borrow multiple dollars in capital markets and can on-lend these leveraged amounts to their borrowers. Thereby, MDBs make efficient use of public funds via multiplying them before on-lending. Importantly, the conditions attached to MDB loans are usually much more favorable to what individual borrowers have direct access to in global capital markets based on their own credit standing. This is possible, centrally, because MDBs themselves can borrow at excellent rates and pass on this advantage to their borrowers. Their prime access to capital markets crucially

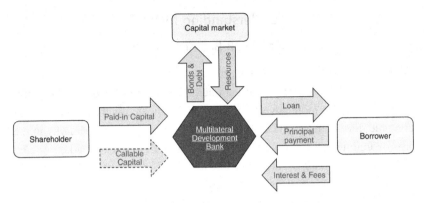

**Figure 1** Financial business model of MDBs
**Source:** Author's figure.

depends on their own creditworthiness, which is regularly assessed and rated by credit rating agencies (CRAs).

## 2.2 Previous International Organizations Literature

Despite the centrality of MDBs' financial model and its uniqueness among IOs, previous MDB research mostly ignores the financial nature of MDBs. Notable exceptions are some, mostly recent, studies that highlight different aspects and consequences of the financial nature of MDBs, such as capital market requirements (Humphrey, 2017a; Munir and Gallagher, 2020), their implications for MDB membership structures (Humphrey, 2016b, 2019), or production and use of net income (Humphrey, 2014; Mohammed, 2004). Very few authors explicitly acknowledge the interdependent duality of MDBs' nature and suggest there to be tensions between the requirements posed by financial markets and the MDB development mandate (Bazbauers and Engel, 2021; Ben-Artzi, 2016; Gutner, 2002). These authors share with this Element the assumption that the development and the financial natures of MDBs are interlinked. Yet, neither of them explicitly theorizes or empirically investigates this interlinkage and its implications.

Today, IOs are widely perceived in academic literature as actors in their own right, with a certain degree of agency, both in the rationalist (Hawkins et al., 2006a) and constructivist (Barnett and Finnemore, 2004) camps of IO research as well as in the International Public Administration literature (Bauer et al., 2017; Oestreich, 2012). These approaches toward IOs share the assumption that IOs are responsive to their environment, for reasons including the acquisition of material resources necessary for organizational survival as well as legitimation processes with external audiences (cf. Barnett and Coleman, 2005).

Relatedly, pertinent MDB research shows MDBs as strategic and powerful actors in their own right, with certain degrees of autonomy vis-à-vis their member states (Lyne et al., 2006; Park and Weaver, 2012; Schneider and Tobin, 2011; Weaver, 2008). The theoretical argument developed in Section 3 has some touch points with the Principal-Agent (PA) framework, which has been repeatedly applied to the MDB context. It stipulates that member states delegate tasks and authority[1] to IOs, and monitor and control them to avoid opportunistic behavior by international bureaucracies (Hawkins et al., 2006a). The PA framework is applied primarily for the purpose of examining and explaining gaps between IO mandates and their actual behavior, also called agency slack (Hawkins et al., 2006b).

Scholars have developed extensions of the classical PA theory to better fit it to MDBs, where authority is never delegated by a single principal. Instead, collective or multiple principals are usually involved here (Nielson and Tierney, 2003, p. 247; termed "complex principals" in Lyne et al., 2006). In such cases, agency slack can occur in face of preference heterogeneity or power asymmetries among principals (Nielson and Tierney, 2003; Sobol, 2016). Another extension to the PA framework – antinomic delegation – is defined as "delegation consisting of conflicting or complex tasks that are difficult to institutionalize and implement", which poses challenges to "agents ... trying to implement goals that are difficult to specify and/or juggle" (Gutner, 2005, p. 11). Hence, Gutner expects performance problems from conflicting or overly complex tasks being delegated from member states to MDBs.

Two elements of PA framework mitigate its applicability to the conceptualization of the dual nature of MDBs: First, at the heart of PA theory lies the delegation relationship between the principal and the agent, which always includes a conditional grant (and potential revocation) of authority from one distinct actor (the principal) to another (the agent) (Hawkins et al., 2006b, p. 7). Member states are the only discrete actors with preferences and deliberate control mechanisms in a position of delegating authority to IOs. Therefore, they are IOs' sole plausible principals, which limits PA-theory's perspective on actors influencing IO behavior to member states. Potentially, this is one reason for previous MDB literature's neglect of the financial pressures exerted by financial markets, which are neither a distinct, nor a state actor with the authority to formally delegate to MDBs.

Second, the PA framework focuses on whether, to which extent, and why IOs do or do not deviate from their principals' preferences and usually assumes opportunistic, disloyal, and self-serving agents being responsible for performance

---

[1] Authority is the power of legitimate rule making (cf. Hurd, 1999).

problems (Gutner, 2005, p. 11; Sobol, 2016). Yet, the dual nature of MDBs is not so much about performance problems in the sense of MDB behavior running counter to the interests of member states; nor is it about how member states can control gaps between their preferences and MDB behavior. Instead, MDBs are inherently created as both development and financial organizations and expected by their shareholders to operate as both. Accordingly, the dual MDB nature is neither about opportunistic MDBs, nor about shareholder control, which is, however, where the PA framework has most theoretical leverage.

## 2.3 Contributing to a Better Understanding of MDBs

In line with the contemporary IO literature cited in Section 2.2, in this study, MDBs are conceptualized as actors in their own right. To direct attention to and better understand the dual nature underpinning MDBs' rationality and operations, I analyze MDBs from an institutional logics perspective (Thornton et al., 2015). This elaborate theoretical framework, outlined in the next section, has been developed for and applied to organizational contexts that are in many ways similar to MDBs, such as social enterprises or microfinance organizations (Battilana and Lee, 2014; Zhao and Lounsbury, 2016). It has several overlaps with theoretical (PA) arguments previously developed in IO literature. Yet, given its openness to demands made by nonstate actors and to inherent (contrary to pathologic) complexities, the institutional logics perspective provides analytical leverage for theorizing the complex context MDBs operate in, the challenges arising from competing demands, and the coping mechanisms through which MDBs navigate these complexities.

One of the main contributions of the original research underlying this Element is highlighting the importance of the financial nature of MDBs. I clarify the financial functioning of MDBs and uncover the multiple and opposing demands caused by the dual nature of MDBs on various levels of operation. Thereby, I provide a fuller understanding of MDB operations as being torn between development and financial goals. A conceptual basis for thinking about the distinctive capabilities and limits inflicted by the MDB business model is crucial both for the analysis as well as adequate design of MDB operations. This is widely relevant, as the business model of MDBs has remained largely unchanged over the past seventy years and is common to all twenty-six currently existing MDBs.

Although all MDBs have the same basic operational model, it is too simplistic to assume all of them to be "mini-World Banks" (cf. Park and Strand, 2016, p. 15). This Element's perspective extends beyond the World Bank, which so far has received the vast majority of academic attention. MDB research usually focuses on a single or small number of MDBs. Instead, in this Element, I introduce a comprehensive definition of MDBs, develop an argument that applies to the entire universe of MDBs, and empirically test hypotheses derived from it in a comparative setting, using an originally collected longitudinal dataset on lending patterns and financial indicators of fifteen MDBs. I propose and show the value of a new typology of MDBs, which can be utilized to classify the universe of MDBs and to better understand their behavior in various contexts beyond the research underlying this Element.

This is an innovative and inherently interdisciplinary work: a neglected, yet globally relevant subject in International Relations (IR) studies is explored by leveraging a theory that originates in organizational sociology and helps uncover complex trade-offs at play in IO operations, as well as an empirical approach from management studies. DEA is especially appropriate for the empirical analysis of organizational performance in settings characterized by small numbers of organizations and multidimensional goals, which frequently is the case in IO research. By importing the institutional logics perspective as well as DEA to IO research, by illustrating their applicability, and highlighting their virtues, this Element can considerably advance the study of IO operations and performance beyond MDBs.

## 3 Theorizing the Dual Nature of MDBs

### 3.1 Institutional Logics and Institutional Complexity

Institutional logics are organizing principles guiding individual and organizational actors in their behavior (Reay and Hinings, 2009). These logics shape the "formal and informal rules of action, interaction, and interpretation" and hence "guide and constrain decision makers in accomplishing the organization's tasks" (Thornton and Ocasio, 1999, p. 804). Institutional logics shape interests, identities, values, beliefs, rules, goals, and thereby ultimately structure the behavior of actors: On the one side, they guide actors' interpretation of external stimuli, perceptions of relevance, and attention to potential responses. In addition, actors align their interests, goals, and behavior with the demands arising from the institutional logic followed by other relevant actors, in anticipation of the potential consequences of (not) meeting these demands (Thornton et al., 2012).[2]

---

[2] To an IR audience, the concept of the institutional logic might evoke that of the international regime, which is defined as "principles, norms, rules, and decision-making procedures around which actors' expectations converge in a given issue area" (Krasner, 1983, p. 2). Yet, specific areas of international action are usually controlled by only one international regime, which is the result of actors' converging interests. This leaves little theoretical leverage for a case, as with the MDBs, of two competing forces.

Actors who are embedded in a given institutional logic, who therefore support it and stipulate compliance with its demands, are termed its institutional referents (Bertels and Lawrence, 2016, p. 339; Vermeulen et al., 2016, p. 280). These are similar to what is called stakeholders in political science literature: As the proponents of a certain institutional logic, institutional referents induce other actors in their issue area to behave according to this logic's demands. They promote, disseminate, monitor, and pressure other actors to adopt logic-consistent behavior via the conferring or withdrawal of key resources and legitimacy (Greenwood et al., 2011, p. 318; Pache and Santos, 2010, p. 458). Institutional referents can be, for example, major funders, accreditation agencies, professional organizations with normative socialization power, or regulatory bodies enacting legal power (Pache and Santos, 2010, p. 457).

Institutional processes shape organizational behavior primarily in the organizational field (see Pache and Santos, 2010, p. 457), which consists of interdependent actors in a recognized area of institutional life (DiMaggio and Powell, 1983, p. 148). The field of multilateral development banking comprises the twenty-six MDBs as well as various stakeholders, such as MDB shareholder governments,[3] investors, borrowers, CRAs, and civil society organizations, who all function as institutional referents shaping the goals, interests, and behavior of MDBs. Just as other IOs, MDBs need to comply with the demands of institutional referents in control of important tangible and intangible resources, to secure legitimacy and authority and to gain tangibles that ensure organizational survival and security (Barnett and Coleman, 2005; Tallberg and Zürn, 2019). By now, the MDB stage is relatively crowded and consequentially the potential for competition among MDBs is growing (Kellerman, 2019; Weaver, 2008, p. 63), which further increases the necessity to be responsive to prescriptions advanced by important institutional referents.

Here, the institutional complexity literature builds on the thinking of Pfeffer and Salancik's (1978) Resource Dependence theory, which provides helpful analytical tools to identify relevant state and nonstate institutional referents and their power dynamics, and to map (conflicting) institutional demands (Ocasio and Gai, 2020, p. 269; Wry et al., 2013). The larger an actor's dependence on (im)material resources by an institutional referent, the higher the latter's influence over the former to comply with the institutional demands arising from their

---

[3] Similar to what is common in PA, constructivist, and International Public Administration approaches, MDB shareholders are treated here as separate from MDB management, which has considerable levels of autonomy vis-à-vis MDB boards (Gutner, 2005; Lyne et al., 2009; Nielson and Tierney, 2003).

supported institutional logic. At this point, the institutional logics perspective has some overlaps with PA theory, with respect to one actor seeking to control another's behavior according to the former's expectations. Yet, as stated in Section 2, PA theory is based very much on the formal transfer of authority, principals' control over agents, and divergent agent behavior. In contrast, the institutional logics perspective not only expects complexities but also allows to integrate nonstate actors making (conflicting) demands as well as provides theoretical arguments for organizational responses toward complexities.

Usually, the actions and interactions in one organizational field are guided by one dominant institutional logic, which can, however, over time be replaced by another. An example is how the dominant logic in the field of higher education publishing shifted from a professional editorial logic to a commercial market logic in the 1970s, each with their respective demands and prescriptions to publishing houses (Thornton and Ocasio, 1999). Recently, scholars have become increasingly interested in understanding the implications of the coexistence of multiple institutional logics in a given organizational field (Besharov and Smith, 2014; Greenwood et al., 2011; Kraatz and Block, 2008; Pache and Santos, 2013; Vermeulen et al., 2016), which also is the case for MDBs, as shown in Sections 3.2 and 3.3.

## 3.2 The Development and Financial Logics

MDBs occupy a unique location "at the intersection of the international development system and the international financial system" and therefore "interact with most of the actors in both systems" (Sagasti and Prada, 2006, p. 68). As a result, MDBs are embedded in a development and a financial institutional logic in nonconcessional development lending, which is their core organizational activity. Each of these two logics prescribes a unique goal, considers various tools appropriate, prescribes different behavior to gain legitimacy form again different key institutional referents, as presented in Table 1. MDB lending operations involve the project, portfolio, policy, and governance levels (cf. Ebrahim and Herz, 2011) and while the subsequent theoretical framework illustrates how the two institutional logics play out on each of them, the empirical analysis in the next section zooms in on the portfolio level. In addition to institutional demands stipulated by external institutional referents, MDB officials usually come from a variety of professional backgrounds, each again embedded in a certain institutional logic shaping identities and goals of individuals. Yet, I here concentrate on how the institutional demands of external institutional referents shape MDB behavior, and hence give less attention to MDB staff and officials acting as institutional referents.

**Table 1** Characteristics of development and financial logics in development lending

| Characteristics | Development logic | Financial logic |
|---|---|---|
| Prescribed goal | Long-term economic development in member states | Financial viability of MDB |
| Objectives | Overcome market failures, meet funding demands not met by private capital market | Increase profits and manage financial risks |
| Source of output legitimacy | Social value: collective welfare gains, distributive fairness, protection of rights, contribution to the SDGs, no harm to locals (among others) | Economic value: high rate of return, low credit risk (as indicated by high credit rating) |
| Expected lending behavior | Maximize overall lending volume, allocation of funds according to need and effective use, setting favorable lending conditions, elaborate social and environmental safeguards | Adherence to prudent banking standards, generating net income, hold capital cushion, balanced risk-return-ratios, quick and flexible project cycles |
| Key institutional referents | (Borrowing) Member states, civil society organizations | Credit rating agencies, investors, member states |
| Illustrative MDB statements (examples) | ". . . reduce poverty and improve living conditions and quality of life" (ADB, 2008, p. 1) | "Consistent track record of profitability since 2004" (BSTDB, 2020b) |
| | ". . . have a significant positive social, economic and environmental impact" (IIB, 2021) | "A consistent triple-A credit rating based on excellent financial performance" (IFC, 2021) |
| | ". . . supporting efforts to reduce poverty and inequality" (IDB, 2021) | "The EDB's priority is to establish long-term and trustworthy relationships with various types of investors" (EDB, 2021) |

**Source:** Author's own compilation based on dimensions identified by Pache and Santos (2013, p. 980) and Thornton et al. (2012).

### 3.2.1 The Development Logic

The development logic's main goal derives from MDBs' mission of fostering the (socio)economic development of member states. The key rationale for the existence of MDBs and the main justification for their nonconcessional development lending activities is the compensation for (capital) market imperfections (Gilbert et al., 2006, p. 47). MDBs are expected to extend loans at favorable conditions to contexts where social returns usually surpass economic returns, that is, to countries, policies, sectors, and projects that are, due to lacking adequate information and elevated risk levels involved, not at all or only insufficiently reached by private capital markets. Economic development is a broad concept, leaving room for a range of activities and ways to pursue it, and potentially depending on the respective prevalent development paradigm of the time. Accordingly, the specific demands arising from the development logic tend to be elusive and challenging to specify.

MDBs' key institutional referents granting them resources and legitimacy based on their adherence to the development logic's demands are their shareholders. They can affect MDB behavior through financial contributions, formal board representation and informal influence (Babb, 2009; Kilby, 2006; Wade, 2002) and have enshrined the development logic in MDB mandates. The relevance of the development logic becomes apparent in every MDBs' mission statement, as exemplified by that of the IBRD – "reduce poverty and build shared prosperity" (IBRD, 2020), the BSTDB – "foster economic growth and regional cooperation amongst its Member States" (BSTDB, 2020a) or the AfDB – "contribute to the sustainable economic development and social progress of its regional members" (AfDB, 2016, p. 2). Accordingly, member states expect MDBs to engage in lending operations in ways that do justice to their mandates and foster their core goals.

Besides member states, civil society organizations are key proponents of the development logic. Civil society groups have over the last decades become increasingly engaged in various activities and stages of the policy cycle, assuming monitoring and whistle-blowing functions. Today, they are crucial to MDBs for normative legitimacy (Park, 2010; Weaver, 2008, p. 65) and MDBs therefore need to be receptive to the demands of civil society groups (Ebrahim and Herz, 2011; Park, 2010; Schettler, 2020). Broadly speaking, in the perspective of civil society organizations, MDBs are expected to be inclusive and responsive to the poor, to defend their rights, improve their equitable access to resources and opportunities, and to achieve positive social and environmental impacts with their operations (Ebrahim and Herz, 2011, p. 60). Beyond that, the number of development logic referents and their influence over MDBs are growing, potentially including academic organizations and the broader development community (Gutner, 2017, p. 142), private foundations (Sagasti and Prada, 2006, p. 98) as well as MDBs' independent evaluation groups (Weaver, 2008, pp. 66–69). However, these are not covered here in more detail, as shareholders and civil society groups by themselves are relevant enough to make this logic key to MDBs.

### 3.2.2 The Financial Logic

MDBs, and this sets them apart from other IOs, are financially self-sustaining organizations. Even though their main goal is not profit maximization and they do not usually distribute surpluses to their shareholders, their financial model evokes a financial logic, which is related to the market logic specified in other contexts (cf. Zhao and Lounsbury, 2016, p. 648). Yet, it deviates from it for the main reason that MDBs' primary goal is not profit maximization. Just as other not-for-profit organizations (Bowman, 2011; Weisbrod, 1998b), MDBs nevertheless need to secure financial profitability, efficiency, and stability. To ensure organizational survival, which MDBs (just as any other organization) have a built-in, overriding interest in, they must ensure sufficient inward flows to cover their costs. Financial integrity hence is key to the functioning and survival of MDBs and one of their key concerns (Sagasti and Prada, 2006, pp. 90, 103). The main prescription of the financial logic is maintaining financial viability, that is, "the financial capacity [the] mission requires and sustaining it over time" (Bowman, 2011, p. 1), including the capacity to attract the capital required to repay creditors based on own performance (Thorne and Du Toit, 2009, p. 687).

Key referents conferring resources upon operational behavior in line with the financial logic are MDB member states, CRAs, and investors. Accordingly, MDB are "paying obsessively close attention to their financial results" (Humphrey, 2016b, p. 94) and "credit ratings have been at the core of the business model of many MDBs" (G20, 2015). MDBs primarily fund their operations with borrowings from international capital markets, retained earnings, and repayments from borrowers. All these funding sources require adherence to sound banking principles and the incorporation of market-based criteria into MDB operations.

First, the operative capacity of MDBs crucially relies on obtaining low enough borrowing costs to have a funding cost advantage to pass on to borrowers. Even after adding a small mark-up to cover administrative costs, loans need to be affordable and attractive to MDB borrowers. MDB borrowing costs are a function of investors' confidence in bonds' security of investment, that is, an appropriate balance between risk and return of investments.

Competing for capital with sovereigns, private corporations, and financial organizations, MDBs need to pay close attention to their repayment capacity, generate revenue for existing investors, and achieve returns to attract new investments. The need to secure low borrowing costs translates into MDBs' efforts for high credit ratings, which are accorded by CRAs and are an expression of the creditworthiness of an issuing entity or a debt instrument. The most prominent CRAs, and most important to MDBs, are the "Big Three": S&P, Fitch, and Moody's. They regularly assess MDBs' financial strength based on a range of indicators, including capital adequacy, leverage, profitability, and liquidity. CRAs in essence act as "capital market gatekeepers" and "have a very powerful role in shaping the perceptions of many bond investors who do not have the time and information to easily evaluate debt securities themselves – particularly MDBs, about which most bond investors know little" (Humphrey, 2017a, pp. 285–286).

Second, despite not being classical profit maximizing organizations, MDBs strive for positive net income for a variety of reasons. It is generated from loan interest rates and fees, and to a smaller degree from MDBs' own investment activities, minus total expenses. MDB net income is usually not distributed as dividends to shareholders and exempt from corporate income tax. It can hence be fully retained and allocated to other purposes. On the one hand, net income can be used as a financial contribution to concessional lending arms or special and trust funds. Cross-financing funds with earnings from nonconcessional MDB lending is in the interests particularly of nonborrowing members, who then need to provide fewer budgetary contributions themselves (Humphrey and Michaelowa, 2013, p. 153; Mohammed, 2004).

On the other hand, net income can be allocated to financial reserves to build up equity (consisting of accumulated earnings and paid-in capital), thereby strengthening an MDB's capital position. As such, it provides a buffer against the depletion of an MDB's capital base and thus serves as an additional reassurance to bond holders, which can help reduce funding costs. Also, growing equity through retained earnings reduces the risks of a call on callable capital, a measure of last resort that both MDBs and their shareholders are keen to avoid. Up to now, no MDB has ever made a capital call, a step that would certainly entail devastating consequences by harming the MDB's and the MDB system's reputation, downgrading its debt, and possibly even causing its closing (Delikanli et al., 2018, p. 37; Kapur and Raychaudhuri, 2014, p. 3; Mistry, 1995, p. 166). In addition, building up equity through net income is the easiest and most effective way to accumulate usable capital, being by far less complex and time-consuming than convincing shareholders of a capital increase (Humphrey, 2014, pp. 625–626) and shields MDBs against political interference by member states, which frequently is exerted during negotiations surrounding capital increases (Babb, 2009; Woods, 2006).

## 3.3 MDBs Operating under Volatile Complexity

Institutional complexity is present in an organizational field when its organizations face "incompatible prescriptions from multiple influential institutional logics" (Greenwood et al., 2011, p. 317). Operating under institutional complexity creates dilemmas, tensions, and challenges for organizations (Greenwood et al., 2011; Raynard, 2016): When competing demands arise from multiple institutional logics, simultaneous compliance with them is impossible, which creates confusion and conflict, and can jeopardize the legitimacy, resources, and social support from important institutional referents (Battilana and Lee, 2014, p. 410; Pache and Santos, 2010, p. 456, 2013, p. 973). Being dependent on institutional referents and the resources they provide, both tangible and intangible, organizational survival in the context of institutional complexity requires organizations to carefully navigate this complexity by deciding which of the multiple institutional demands to satisfy, to alter, or to dismiss (Greenwood et al., 2011; Pache and Santos, 2010; Raynard, 2016).

Dealing with multiple institutional referents promoting two distinct institutional logics, as shown in Section 3.2, and operating in complex material and normative environments (cf. Weaver, 2008, p. 30), MDBs are particularly prone to complexities in which conflicting pressures cannot easily be reconciled. More specifically, MDBs operate in a context of what is termed volatile institutional complexity. Compared to the restrained and segregated types of institutional complexity, volatile complexity is the most difficult for organizations to navigate (Raynard, 2016). It is the result of three factors: First, multiple logics have jurisdictional overlap, that is, intersect at several decision points close to the operational core (Besharov and Smith, 2014, pp. 368–369; Raynard, 2016, p. 314). Second, a field's level of centralization, that is, the power structure between institutional referents, is decisive for the type of institutional complexity present. Highly centralized fields have one dominant institutional referent, who establishes a clear hierarchy between multiple logics, compels consensus around that hierarchy, and resolves disagreement. The result would be a relatively clear prioritization of logics' demands (Pache and Santos, 2010, p. 457; Raynard, 2016, pp. 313–314). In contrast, organizational fields characterized by volatile institutional complexity are moderately centralized, consisting of multiple misaligned, relatively powerful, and nondominant institutional referents (Pache and Santos, 2010, p. 458). Third is logic incompatibility, which is the defining characteristic of institutional complexity and arises when compliance with the demands of one institutional logic precludes compliance with the demands posed by the other logic(s) (Raynard, 2016, p. 313). The degree of incompatibility increases with the number of uncoordinated institutional referents (Pache and Santos, 2010, p. 457), with the complexity of tasks performed (Besharov and Smith, 2014, p. 369), and the room for interpretation of, negotiation of, and discretion over institutional demands (Raynard, 2016, p. 313).

The three factors stated in the previous paragraph are all present in the field of MDBs: Their organizational core is extending nonconcessional loans, where the development and financial logic are both highly relevant. Here, the two simultaneously aim at a range of crucial aspects of lending, among them loan conditions, internal processes, or portfolio structures, as shown in the subsequent paragraphs. Second, the field of multilateral development banking is characterized by moderate centralization, as a small number of important and powerful institutional referents is involved. These are nonborrowing member states, providing the majority of paid-in and callable capital; borrowing member states, contributing capital, holding sway over loan repayment, and upholding demand for MDB loans; civil society groups, granting legitimacy to MDBs for their development operations; CRAs, providing much-needed credit ratings; and investors and bond holders, supplying operating funds at favorable conditions. Among these, member states certainly are the only actors with formalized authority over MDBs and research clearly shows the formal and informal influence especially of large nonborrowing states (among many others, e.g. Babb, 2009; Dreher et al., 2009; Kersting and Kilby, 2021; Kilby, 2006). Yet, given that MDBs do have some degrees of autonomy vis-à-vis their members (Bauer and Ege, 2017; Park and Weaver, 2012), they are subjected to the influence of multiple, including nonstate, players, whose influence is potent enough to be imposed on the MDBs (cf. Pache and Santos, 2010, p. 458). Importantly, member states do not have any authority over the other institutional referents in the field and therefore cannot arbitrate and resolve disagreement between them. Third, regarding logic incompatibility, the demands arising from the development and financial logics aimed at the core lending activities are not only overlapping but conflicting in many instances.[4]

This conflictual relationship arises on all operational levels, as is subsequently illustrated. On the project level, embeddedness in the development or financial logic implies varied types of loans, projects, and sectors as well as different approaches to loan conditions. For instance, in the financial logic, projects are

---

[4] I chose to use the term "conflicting" instead of "incompatible," which is frequently used in the institutional logics literature, because the demands of the development and the financial logic certainly are not entirely incompatible, given that they have both been present in multilateral development banking for decades.

preferred to be financially attractive and bankable (Gutner, 2002, p. 108), ideally self-liquidating by producing tangible economic rates of return and yielding fast and high output and productivity increases to repay the debt. These are usually projects in "hard" infrastructural and productive sectors, such as power plants, dams, roads, and machinery. However, this might come at the cost of attention to social and human development issues, which are sought by actors in the development logic (Alacevich, 2008, pp. 2–10; Weaver, 2008, p. 60). A focus on low-risk and profitable MDB projects can also crowd out local private sector lenders (Humphrey, 2019, p. 181). Loans to social sectors and institutional development are usually smaller, more laborious, and more time-intensive (Institute of Development Studies, 2000, pp. 70–71), increasing administrative expenses, which yet again counters financial efficiency aspirations.

Actors in the two logics also prefer different loan conditions, including terms for interest rates and fees as well as maturity and grace periods. In the financial logic, loan charges need to be set to a maximum level within the boundaries of borrower demand (determined by borrower affordability and international creditor competition), to ensure high net income. In addition, loans would be priced according to financial risks, as is standard in commercial banking. In the financial logic. maturity and grace periods are short to reduce risks and uncertainty, but high enough to maintain demand by borrowers, considering international competition (cf. Humphrey, 2014). In the development logic, on the other side, loan charges are extremely low, so that borrowers can put their resources to developmentally more beneficial uses than interest or fee payment. Risk-based pricing would be refused to ensure equitable and affordable access to MDB loans to borrowers with various levels of credit risk, especially those most in need. Broadly put, in the development logic, MDB maturity and grace periods are as long as necessary to allow for the effective realization of long-term development projects and loans are extended under conditions by which they do not compete with or crowd out private sector lending.

On the portfolio level, regarding its overall volume, in the financial logic, MDBs would hold a sufficiently large capital cushion against unexpected losses when extended loans become impaired. However, higher cushions limit MDBs' operational scope, whereby, according to the development logic, overall lending volumes should be expanded to a maximum. For example, an increase in the IDB's debt-to-equity ratio of 2.8× by 0.2× to 3.0× could increase its business volume by almost USD 6 billion, a similar increase in the debt ratio at AfDB, from 3.3× to 3.5×, would increase AfDB's business volume by USD 1 billion.[5]

---

[5] Based on AfDB and IDB's 2018 debt and equity, calculated assuming a third of increased debt to be held as cash and two thirds lent as assets (cf. method by Kapur and Raychaudhuri, 2014, p. 21).

While this is in line with the development logic, it is not with the financial logic, for reasons of jeopardizing credit ratings and investors' confidence in MDBs' financial standing.

Similarly, the two logics' demands are discordant regarding portfolio composition of eligible borrowers. Contrary to most concessional MDB lending, usually relying on so-called performance-based allocation (PBA), the distribution of nonconcessional MDB lending is not determined by such formulas, leaving more discretion in its configuration. In the development logic, loans would be extended to contexts most harshly hit by market failures like unmet demand or untenable lending conditions. These are, by tendency, countries with higher financial risk, where private financing is scarce (Arvanitis et al., 2015, p. 196; Kharas and Noe, 2018, pp. 16, 18; Moody's, 2019, p. 6; Woods, 2006, p. 9). Given their mandated quest for social, and not just economic returns, in the development logic MDBs are in essence expected to be financial "risk lovers", who in financial jargon are "willing to accept lower expected returns on prospects with higher amounts of risk" (Lee and Lee, 2013, p. 164). Yet, in the financial logic, less risky portfolios are preferable, since this – considering that capital cushions are directly linked to portfolio riskiness – increases the feasible absolute volume of exposures and thus potential earnings through payment of charges, especially when risk-based pricing is not exercised. Also, it minimizes expected losses and requires less provisioning, which in turn secures the steady accumulation of reserves via retained earnings. Contrastingly, higher-risk portfolios can erode MDBs' capital bases, both through losses from nonperforming loans and higher provisioning requirements. Equity being set (which usually cannot be increased on short notice), a high-risk portfolio would also result in downgrades. Furthermore, in the development logic, there would be increased countercyclical lending in times of economic downturns; actors in the financial logic discourage precisely that, as lending to countries facing rating pressures makes lending to them more expensive in terms of capital consumption (Avellán and Galindo, 2018).

Following the two logics also implies different policies. In the financial logic, loans are extended quickly and flexibly within short project cycles, to keep the money flowing (Rich, 2013, p. 56). Also, management efficiency would be maximized by limiting administrative, personnel and other overhead costs (Grier, 2012, p. 36). In the development logic, contrarily, project appraisal, safeguard requirements, and loan conditionality are comprehensive and elaborate to limit negative and strengthen positive development results (Delikanli et al., 2018, p. 28; Ebrahim and Herz, 2011, p. 66; Humphrey, 2016a, 2019). While risk management departments have a powerful role during the project cycle in the financial logic, country experts would be in charge in the development logic. As another example, the IBRD's charter expects lending without regard to political considerations to secure investor confidence (Kapur et al., 1997, p. 8), which limits development-oriented attention to good governance and corruption (Gutner, 2017, p. 156).

Finally, the two logics diverge regarding their governance-level demands. Weighted voting similar to what is frequent practice in commercial organizations, systems of shared board seats, and, at some MDBs, presidents always coming from a nonborrowing country tend to favor wealthier, nonborrowing members (Ebrahim and Herz, 2011, p. 73; Vestergaard and Wade, 2013). This is much more in line with the financial logic because nonborrowers tend to be financially more conservative and smaller boards (by grouping shareholders into constituencies) financially advisable (cf. Mair et al., 2015, p. 717). Yet, these arrangements can undermine MDB development impact, by neglecting the voice of countries most directly affected by board decisions, weakening MDBs' legitimacy as representative organizations, and discouraging necessary financial contributions of middle-income countries (Birdsall, 2014, p. 3; Griffith-Jones, 2002, p. 1).

In sum, behavior implied to the lending operations of MDBs in the two logics oftentimes is discordant, at all levels from a single project to governance arrangements. Combined with the two logics' overlapping at the MDB operational core and a lacking hierarchy among key referents, as described at the beginning of this section, this results in MDBs operating under volatile institutional complexity, which needs to be coped with but is particularly challenging to navigate (cf. Raynard, 2016, p. 324).

## 3.4 Crafting a Compromise between the Logics

As stated Section 3.3, institutional complexity causes tensions and challenges that organizations need to navigate to ensure organizational capacity and survival. The feasibility and choice of different organizational responses to institutional complexity are driven primarily by the specific type of complexity present (Besharov and Smith, 2014; Raynard, 2016). In case of the volatile institutional complexity faced by MDBs, neither is the manipulation of logics (in a way they no longer make conflicting demands) possible (Kraatz and Block, 2008, p. 251; Ocasio and Radoynovska, 2016, p. 300; Oliver, 1991, pp. 157–158; Pache and Santos, 2010, p. 463); nor is elimination of logics via outright rejection, through "window dressing"–like concealment of noncompliance, or through decoupling tactics feasible (Greenwood et al., 2011, p. 350; Kraatz and Block, 2008, p. 250; Oliver, 1991, pp. 154–155; Pache and Santos, 2013, p. 974).

The main reason for the infeasibility of elimination and manipulation is that both logics are enshrined in MDB mandates, and thus inescapable. This is different to most other organizations which are usually voluntarily embedded in certain logics. In addition, the MDBs' organizational field is by now relatively mature, giving its institutional referents strong enough ties into the MDBs to channel prescriptions and to scrutinize sufficient conformity with institutional demands. Manipulation or elimination tactics, for example in the form of shifting either their development tasks or their financial obligations as borrowers to peripheral subunits, would entail discontent, social penalties, and withdrawal of support (cf. Greenwood et al., 2011, 343, 337; Pache and Santos, 2013, p. 974). Accordingly, for several decades, MDBs have existed without the substantial changes to the fundamental development mandate or business model that would indicate manipulation or elimination (cf. Heldt and Schmidtke, 2019). Instead, MDBs can only resort to compromising between development and financial logics.

The only kind of organizational response to institutional complexity feasible to MDBs is thus crafting a compromise between multiple diverging logics, by complying to minimum standards with each and bargaining with or pacifying merely partly satisfied institutional referents to not lose their support (Kraatz and Block, 2008, p. 251; Oliver, 1991, p. 154; Pache and Santos, 2010, p. 462). Like a scale, this compromise can tilt toward either side when more relative importance is granted to the demands of one logic, while always ensuring minimum fulfillment of additional, opposing institutional demands.

Interestingly, this pattern of prioritization among the logics does not need to be uniform across organizations in an organizational field, since field-level institutional pressures can be experienced and assessed, and hence acted upon, differently by the organizations comprising it (Goodrick and Reay, 2011, p. 399; Greenwood et al., 2011; Ocasio and Radoynovska, 2016, p. 296; Pache and Santos, 2010, p. 458). Which logic is prioritized depends on each logic's proponents' influence over important tangible and intangible resources (Greenwood et al., 2011, p. 349; Oliver, 1991; see also Pache and Santos, 2010; Pfeffer and Salancik, 1978). In addition, the specific demands prescribed by institutional referents can vary across organizations; and certain organizational characteristics, such as structure, ownership, and governance, can make individual organizations more or less sensitive to certain logics than others (Greenwood et al., 2011, p. 319). As a consequence, among actors in a given field, there can be "stable differences" (Cobb et al., 2016, p. 2104) in their respective configurations of compromise. This allows to uncover potential variation in the specific patterns of compromise reached across the MDBs.

### 3.4.1 Variation along Portfolio Composition

The first dimension I expect to be relevant for MDBs' prioritization of the two logics is portfolio composition. MDBs can be divided into two types – those that lend only or predominantly to sovereign borrowers or with sovereign guarantee (S-MDBs) and those that lend exclusively or primarily to private, that is, nonsovereign, borrowers without a sovereign guarantee (P-MDBs). I expect these two types of MDBs to differ in their patterns of compromise.

In S-MDBs, portfolios contain few sovereign borrowers, for which credit risk assessment is relatively straightforward or can be based on CRA ratings. Also, S-MDBs are granted preferential creditor treatment (PCT) by borrowers, meaning that in case of payment difficulties, multilateral is given priority over other debt, which considerably diminishes the risk of default. In contrast, P-MDBs extend loans to numerous private actors, without PCT. Consequently, P-MDBs' loans have a higher risk of default, which leads to (usually) higher nonperforming loans ratios in P-MDBs compared to S-MDBs. In addition, internally estimating the credit risk of multiple private sector actors and to assess sectoral tolerances to avoid systemic risks is challenging. Accounting for these differences, certain institutional referents place stricter financial demands on P-MDBs than S-MDBs, so that P-MDBs need to emphasize the financial logic more strongly than S-MDBs to ensure financial viability.

At the same time, S-MDBs are usually conceived as more intrusive, authoritative, and societally relevant and therefore more publicly scrutinized, contested, and politicized than P-MDBs (cf. Rauh and Zürn, 2020). Consequently, many of the better known MDBs are S-MDBs (like the ADB and AfDB), while less known MDBs mostly are P-MDBs (like the BSTDB and IIB). Similarly, the IBRD and IDB are much more closely observed by civil society than the IFC and IDB Invest, their P-MDB counterparts in the same banking groups. This heightened public awareness of and scrutiny toward S-MDBs are expected to entail stronger demands of adherence to the development logic.

Combined, this leads to the following hypothesis:

> H1: *Private-lending P-MDBs more strongly endorse the financial logic over the development logic than sovereign-lending S-MDBs.*

### 3.4.2 Variation along Shareholder Composition

Second, I expect MDBs' strategic response to institutional complexity to differ with shareholder composition, which can shape "the relative receptivity of organizations to multiple logics" (Greenwood et al., 2011, p. 344). As Humphrey has shown, this variable causally shapes financial considerations of MDBs (2014, p. 633) and it is reasonable to assume it to also be important for MDBs' sensitivity toward the two institutional logics discussed here. MDBs can be separated into two types according to their shareholder composition (Birdsall, 2018; Humphrey, 2014; Ray, 2019), which is a simplification of the complex principals framework developed by Lyne et al. (2009): the first are borrower-dominated MDBs (B-MDBs), in which borrowing member states have over 50 percent of voting power. For instance, the BSDTB belongs to this group, where borrowing member states hold 100 percent of votes. Similarly, at the AfDB and IDB borrowing members hold 59 percent and slightly over 50 percent of voting power. The second type comprises MDBs with a voting majority of nonborrowing creditor countries (C-MDB), including the IBRD and EBRD (34 percent and 11 percent of votes held by borrowers). This variable is important as the preferences of members, although comprising different countries with various interests, tend to converge within and diverge between shareholder groups (Humphrey and Michaelowa, 2013, p. 144).

For several reasons, creditor member states have a larger interest than borrowing members in prioritizing the financial logic. To them, it makes a substantial difference whether business growth is paid for through earnings or shareholder capital contributions. In the former, it is mainly the borrowing members who pay for equity expansions through loan charges; on the contrary, nonborrowers usually pay for large parts of general capital increases, without directly benefitting from them (Humphrey, 2014, p. 628). In addition, nonborrowers usually have pledged much larger shares of callable capital and therefore have a more vital interest in preventing a call on these sizeable sums. In C-MDBs, I therefore expect nonborrowing members to impose a greater emphasis on the financial logic (see also Humphrey, 2019, pp. 182, 186).

In contrast, in B-MDBs it does not make such a difference whether capital is grown via earnings or capital contributions. As in a cooperative, funds are provided by the same circle of members who eventually benefit from them, so that shareholders are often more willing to inject new capital and need to focus less strictly on financial achievements. This is also what is expected by S&P. B-MDBs usually receive a rating discount against the expectation that they adhere less stringently to the principle of financial viability than demanded by investors (see, for instance, S&P, 2019, pp. 44, 147). Instead, B-MDBs tend to have closer ties with their borrowers, which makes them open to act flexibly upon development needs (Humphrey, 2019, p. 183; cf. Humphrey and Michaelowa, 2013, p. 145). Less pressure to adhere to the financial logic and larger incentives to attend to development needs are expected to cause a larger focus on the development logic at B-MDBs. This leads to the following hypothesis:

H2: *Creditor-dominated C-MDBs more strongly endorse the financial logic over the development logic than borrower-dominated B-MDBs.*

In this section, I have introduced the main concepts and arguments of the institutional logics perspective. Scholars of institutional complexity expect organizations operating in fields characterized by conflicting institutional logics that overlap at the organizational core and lack a field-level hierarchy to be exposed to volatile institutional complexity, which needs to be managed through organizational response strategies. I have shown the volatile institutional complexity present in the field of multilateral development banking and argued that MDB navigate it by striking a compromise between the development and financial logics. Based on this, I derived two hypotheses on the varying patterns of relative prioritization of these two logics at distinct types of MDBs.

## 4 Analyzing Institutional Compliance

Empirically assessing hypotheses on differentiated MDB responses toward volatile institutional complexity requires operationalizing and comparing MDB behavior to institutionally demanded behavior. To this end, the following analysis is based on the ideal types technique described by Reay and Jones (2016). The distance between institutionally expected ideal-typical behavior and actual behavior is measured using Data Envelopment Analysis (DEA), which, other advantages, can accommodate the multidimensionality and intangibility of institutional demands. The chosen methodological approach enables systematic comparison across several MDBs.

### 4.1 The Ideal Type Technique

Ideal types are simplified abstractions of institutional logics with a focus on certain attributes (Ocasio et al., 2017, p. 520), used to "capture" – that is to identify, describe, and measure – mostly elusive institutional logics (Reay and Jones, 2016, p. 442). Actual patterns of behavior are contrasted to ideal types to measure the relative strengths of multiple institutional logics in different organizations. Thereby, it is well suited for systematic analyses of empirical variation, especially in comparative settings and lends itself to the integration of quantitative data (Goodrick and Reay, 2011, p. 382; Ocasio et al., 2017, p. 520; Reay and Jones, 2016, p. 449).

To identify the ideal-typical repertoires of MDB behaviors of both the development and the financial logic, it is necessary to free oneself from reality and to instead specify how MDBs behaved if they were guided only by one certain institutional logic (cf. Goodrick and Reay, 2011, p. 382). To this end, the subsequent empirical analysis zooms in on MDB behavior at the portfolio, that is, the balance sheet, level. Focusing exclusively on a relatively limited domain lets me identify two distinct and empirically observable sets of organizational behaviors in line with what is expected by each logic, based on the pertinent literatures: The normative aid allocation literature on the one, and the banking and not-for-profit organizational literatures on the other side are used to deductively identify the ideal type for each logic. I use the terms "financial performance" to indicate the closeness of actual behavior to that expected by the financial logic and "development performance" for the distance between observed and ideal-typical behavior according to the development logic.[6]

### 4.1.1 Financial Ideal Type

If guided only by the financial logic, MDBs would calibrate their lending portfolio in a way that ensures financial viability. In not-for-profit organizations such as MDBs, this involves more comprehensive measures than in classical profit maximizing organizations (Weisbrod, 1998a, p. 16), where profitability is the primary performance indicator (Bikker and Bos, 2008, p. 26). Therefore, scholars in the not-for-profit literature usually rely on additional accounting constructs, such as liquidity, margin, and solvency, to evaluate financial performance (Prentice, 2016, p. 717; Ryan and Irvine, 2012). This corresponds with more advanced bank financial performance evaluation efforts, such as the CAMELS rating system, using as primary indicators capitalization, asset quality, earnings, and liquidity (Grier, 2012, pp. 18–19). With exception to liquidity, which is the task of treasury and less relevant to MDBs as they do not take deposits, all these factors are subsumed under capital adequacy in CRA methodologies used for MDB ratings. Capital adequacy is a "key consideration for MDBs" and "a critical indicator of an MDB's capacity to absorb credit or market losses stemming from its operations and hence its ability to repay debtholders" (Moody's, 2019, pp. 3, 6). The financial logic's goal of financial viability hence translates into ideal-typical behavior of calibrating the lending portfolio in a way that ensures capital adequacy.

### 4.1.2 Development Ideal Type

Compared to the financial ideal-typical MDB behavior, ideal-typical portfolio composition in line with the development logic is less straightforward. This is because MDBs pursue amorphous goals and provide relatively intangible

---

[6] The term performance is useful when evaluating the 'closeness' of observed to ideal-typical behavior, although it is not frequently used in the institutional logics literature. In organization theory and strategic management, organizational performance is evaluated relative to the agendas or goals set by stakeholders or organizations themselves (Murphy et al., 1996). Accordingly, the "closeness of the usual work practices to the ideal type for each logic" (Goodrick and Reay, 2011, p. 387) can be framed in terms of performance.

services (Gutner and Thompson, 2010, p. 230). However, the comprehensive aid allocation literature provides criteria to specify this ideal type. Given the overarching objective of development impact, when guided only by a development logic, aid agencies should organize their aid giving in ways that ensures the effective translation of the development mission into practice. As they do not have exclusive control over the level of aid effectiveness achieved (Birdsall and Kharas, 2014, pp. 2–3), specifying the development ideal type as the maximization of development effectiveness confounds aid agency behavior with uncontrollable external factors (see also Gutner and Thompson, 2010). In contrast, aid agencies do have full control over the procedural aspect of aid provision, and need to ensure high-quality aid allocation to achieve high aid effectiveness (Tierney et al., 2011, p. 1901). The normative aid allocation literature (cf. McGillivray, 2004)[7] provides well-grounded criteria for high-quality inter-recipient allocation of development assistance, subsumed under the concept of allocative performance, that is, "the desirability of a distribution of a given amount of aid among a given set of potential recipients" (Clist, 2015, p. 808). The relevance of allocative performance is reflected by the common practice in the allocation of MDBs' (and other multilateral agencies') concessional assistance, which usually relies on allocation formulas to determine eligible recipients' shares of assistance, with the purpose of promoting effectiveness and international equity of aid (Guillaumont and Wagner, 2015). The development ideal type hence is a lending portfolio with high-quality inter-recipient loan distribution and accordingly development performance is greater, the more an MDB's assistance meets the relative desirability of recipients (cf. McGillivray, 1989, p. 561).

## 4.2 Data Envelopment Analysis

The closeness of observed to ideal-typical lending reflects the strength of each institutional logic in guiding MDBs' behavior (cf. Reay and Jones, 2016). Capturing this distance is challenging, since each logic's demands are multidimensional and because of MDB missions' high levels of abstraction, intangibles, and lack of output prices. DEA, a nonparametric frontier-based linear programming-based optimization technique (Charnes et al., 1978), is particularly useful in such conditions. Fundamentally, DEA is an efficiency or

---

[7] The aid allocation literature can be divided into positive and normative strands. Within the former, authors identify relevant factors in aid allocation decisions of different donors (Clist, 2011; Vázquez, 2015). Within the normative strand, authors theorize about criteria that should be relevant for aid allocation. Based on these criteria, they either prescribe the optimal allocation of aid per recipient (McGillivray, 2004; Wood, 2008) or assess donor performance in terms of optimal aid allocation patterns (McGillivray, 1989; Roodman, 2012).

performance evaluation tool to compare similar entities using multiple inputs to produce multiple outputs, particularly if these are not measurable in monetary terms. DEA has established itself as a widely used and accepted analytical tool across several disciplines (Emrouznejad and Yang, 2018; Liu et al., 2016). Built on economic production theory, DEA is frequently applied in contexts of private sector firms, oftentimes with a price- and efficiency-based understanding of performance. This can be confusing to audiences outside economics and business research and tends to conceal that DEA has originally been developed for performance assessment of public organizations. For this reason, to depart from private sector terms, the evaluated organizations are called decision-making units (DMUs), which can be public agencies, not-for-profit organizations, industries, firms, or countries (Charnes et al., 1978, p. 429).

Efficiency is the ratio of outputs produced to the inputs used in the process and improves when outputs are increased and/or inputs reduced. As shown in Eq. (1), in a case with multiple inputs and multiple outputs ($x_0 \in \mathbb{R}^m_+$ and $y_0 \, \mathbb{R}^s_+$) the efficiency score $h^*_0$ is given by the ratio of the weighted sum of $s$ outputs to the weighted sum of $m$ inputs (Charnes et al., 1978, p. 430):

$$h^*_0 = max h_0(u,v) = \frac{u_{10}y_{10} + \ldots + u_{s0}y_{s0}}{v_{10}x_{10} + \ldots + v_{mo}x_{mo}} = \frac{\sum_{r=1}^s u_{r0}y_{r0}}{\sum_{i=1}^m v_{i0}x_{i0}} \tag{1}$$

s.t. $\quad \dfrac{\sum_{r=1}^s u_{rj}y_{rj}}{\sum_{i=1}^m v_{ij}x_{ij}} \leq 1; \quad j = 1, \ldots, n,$

$u_{r0}, v_{i0} \geq 0; \qquad r = 1, \ldots, s; \qquad i = 1, \ldots, m,$

with $x_{i0}$ being the amount of input $i$ consumed by $DMU_0$ under evaluation, $y_{r0}$ the amount of output $r$ produced by $DMU_0$; $u_{r0}$ and $v_{i0}$ the DMU-specific weights for the output $r$ and input $i$; $h^*_0$ the relative performance score of $DMU_0$; $x_{ij}$ the amount of input $i$ consumed by DMUs $j$ ($j = 1, \ldots, n$); $y_{rj}$ the amount of output $r$ produced by DMUs $j$ ($j = 1, \ldots, n$). Formulated as the so-called envelopment model, the efficiency scores estimated by DEA represent *relative* efficiency, that is, the efficiency score of a DMU relative to the efficient frontier, which is extrapolated from all efficient DMUs, that is, those in the observed reference set (sample) with the highest ratio, and envelopes all other (the inefficient) DMUs. The relative efficiency score of a DMU then represents the distance of a DMU to the efficient frontier, with efficient DMUs scoring 1 (Charnes et al., 1994, pp. 5–6).

Each DMU receives separate weights for all input and output factors. These weights are given the optimal solution values $u^*_r$, $v^*_i \geq 0$ for each DMU as to maximize its efficiency score $h^*_0$ (Charnes et al., 1978). DEA's unique power is that it does not require ex-ante factor weight specifications, but rather estimates nonnegative weights through an optimization procedure, during which the model is solved $n$ times (once for each DMU) in a way that maximizes each DMU's relative efficiency score (Charnes et al., 1978, p. 431). Hence, DEA presents each DMU in the best possible light, for which reason its weighting procedure is called "Benefit-of-the-Doubt" (BoD) weighting.

In simple words, DEA solves a mathematical optimization procedure multiple times, to find for each DMU that configuration of input and output factor weights, which maximizes the ratio of the weighted sum of outputs to the weighted sum of inputs. The DMUs with the highest efficiencies form the efficient frontier, which envelopes all other DMUs. Each DMU's relative efficiency is then given by the radial distance between this DMU and the frontier.

In recent years, DEA with a single constant input for all DMUs has gained popularity (Karagiannis and Karagiannis, 2018), applied also in composite index construction (Cherchye et al., 2007; van Puyenbroeck and Rogge, 2020). This technique can be used "for comparing any set of homogeneous units on multiple dimensions" (Lovell and Pastor, 1999, p. 46). Here, the denominator of the ratio of weighted outputs to weighted inputs dissolves (being constant across all DMUs), so that relative performance of DMUs is represented by the sum of weighted outputs only. Instead of considering certain input factors, the dummy input is interpreted as a "helmsman" within the DMU pursuing various policy objectives, which are represented by the output factors (Cherchye et al., 2007). Again, output factor weights are BoD weights, with higher weights given to outputs on which a DMU performs (relatively) better to maximize the performance score of each DMU, and relative performance is represented by the distance of a DMU's score to the frontier.

DEA with a constant single input therefore can be used for aggregating several performance subindicators (outputs) without explicit reference to the resources (inputs) used in the process (Karagiannis and Karagiannis, 2018, p. 45). It can serve as a benchmarking or performance evaluation tool for the comparison and classification of similar entities based on a common set of multiple performance attributes (Cook et al., 2014). Disregarding inputs, this particular application of DEA is no longer about efficiency in a strict sense (Cherchye, 2001, p. 408) and it is more precise to speak of best practice instead of efficient DMUs and frontiers (Bendheim et al., 1998; Cook et al., 2014). Also, resulting scores are not efficiency scores, but take a new meaning, depending on the context of application.

DEA, including its constant input version, has several strengths: First, being a nonparametric method, it does not require a priori explicitly formulated assumptions of the distribution of errors or the underlying functional form of the relationship between inputs and outputs, thereby avoiding problems of model mis-specification (Charnes et al., 1994, p. 5; Cooper et al., 2011, p. 2). Equally in contrast to parametric central-tendency methods, such as linear regression, DEA does not make inferences based on average-based coefficient or residual analysis. Instead of estimating a "single optimized regression equation [that] is assumed to apply to each DMU", DEA "optimizes the performance measure of each DMU", which "results in a revealed understanding about each DMU instead of the depiction of a mythical "average" DMU" (Charnes et al., 1994, p. 4). Because DEA focuses on individual instead of average performance, the sample size, which is a critical issue in parametric statistical analysis, is irrelevant in DEA. Hence, DEA is less data demanding compared to parametric approaches and can handle small sample sizes (Cook et al., 2014, p. 2; Lebovics et al., 2016, p. 62). Besides the many advantages inherent in being a nonparametric method, the most frequently stated disadvantage is DEA's susceptibility to sample variation, outliers, and measurement errors (Brown, 2006). However, recent advances in using the bootstrap in DEA have helped define the statistical properties of DEA estimators, minimizing the risks posed by sensitivity to sampling variance (Simar and Wilson, 2011).

One of DEA's most advantageous features is its BoD weighting. For most applications, not needing a priori information about weight specifications is a value in and by itself, as this circumvents problems of subjectivity (Rabar, 2017, p. 1772). Sometimes, even the resulting weights themselves can become the objects of research when considered as indicators of strategic priorities (Cherchye, 2001). At the same time, DEA is flexible enough to accommodate judgment via weight restrictions, when desired (Charnes et al., 1994, p. 8).

In contrast to ratio analysis, the traditional performance evaluation method in the financial sector, DEA can reflect institutional multidimensionality while still providing one aggregated relative performance measure (Charnes et al., 1994, p. 8). It hence avoids many of the conceptual problems inherent in traditional multiple- or single-measure studies of organizational performance (Devinney et al., 2010). DEA can simultaneously accommodate multiple inputs and outputs in different measurement units without the need to standardize data (Charnes et al., 1994, p. 8; Lebovics et al., 2016, p. 62). The resulting performance score is independent of the factors' units of measurement because weights are chosen endogenously and adapt to the units (Cherchye et al., 2007, p. 121). For this reason, DEA is now frequently applied in contexts of organizations with multiple goals and where pricing of products and services is difficult or infeasible – such as social enterprises or microfinance organizations (Reichert, 2018; Staessens et al., 2019).

## 4.3 MDB Development and Financial Performance

DEA with constant single inputs serves well to systematically assess the relative distance of MDB actual to ideal-typical behavior, especially since ideal types are multidimensional and partly nonmonetary. Thereby, it allows to draw conclusions about the relative strengths of coexisting logics across MDBs.

### 4.3.1 Methods

In the following analysis, MDBs serve as the DMUs, each seeking to maximize the levels of certain output factors related to the development or financial logics, as derived in Sections 4.3.3 and 4.3.4 (inputs held constant). MDB financial and development performance each are determined by MDBs' distances relative to the respective best-practice frontier consisting of the best-performing MDBs. The benchmarking standard is thus not based on exogenous criteria but on what is realistic and attainable. This approach results in two aggregate performance measures for each year, one for each institutional logic, which both indicate an MDB's distance from the respective ideal type. Based on these estimates, I conducted correlational, graphical, and statistical analysis to substantiate my assumptions about the conflict between the two institutional logics and to test the hypotheses developed in the previous section. Certainly, this methodological approach cannot establish causality. Yet, it serves well given the novelty of my research question and consequently the lack of (quantitative) empirical material to draw on, the study's comparative aspirations as well as the small number of MDBs. This descriptive evaluative (in ways semiquantitative) approach using nonparametric statistical methods combines the best of both the qualitative and quantitative worlds: It allows for a systematic comparison across several MDBs and the in-depth, substantiated interpretation of results.

Based on the data described in Section 4.3.2, the empirical analysis was conducted using the *deaR* package in *R* (Coll-Serrano et al., 2020). All best-practice frontiers were computed using the output-oriented variable returns to scale specification as developed by Banker et al. (1984).[8] To estimate and correct for potential bias in performance score estimators stemming from sampling variation, especially with a relatively small sample as is the case here, I applied the homogeneous smoothed bootstrap to DEA ($B = 1,000$) as proposed by Simar and Wilson (1998). This way, bias-corrected estimates are obtained, better approximating the unknown real distribution and less sensitive to random errors due to sampling variation and to extreme outliers than uncorrected estimates. Considering that the biases are positive

---

[8] As shown by Lovell and Pastor (1999), the nature of returns of scale is irrelevant in single constant input DEA.

for every observation (meaning that uncorrected estimated are minimally larger than bias-corrected estimates throughout), the use of bootstrapped DEA reduces the risk of over-estimating true MDB performance and ensures greater robustness of results. Also, this approach helps to mitigate the risks of sampling errors in the group-specific analyses.

Hypothesis testing requires a measure of MDBs' relative prioritization of logics. Given that true relative prioritization patterns are unknown, they are inferred here from MDBs' observed strengths and weaknesses. High performance on one institutional logic is treated as an indicator for high priority of that logic. Against this backdrop, an intuitive priority measure is the ratio of the development to the financial performance score, which can be mathematically deduced through the marginal rate of transformation of outputs (MRT). This measures the "rate at which a DMU willingly exchanges an amount of one production factor for another one" (Sueyoshi and Yuan, 2016, p. 275). Given that factor weights assigned in DEA can be considered to reflect policy priorities (Cherchye, 2001, pp. 408, 415; Cherchye et al., 2007; Prior and Surroca, 2006, p. 297), the MRT is equal to the ratio of weights attributed to two factors in the course of BoD weighting (Banker et al., 1984; Sueyoshi and Yuan, 2016). In this analysis, interest is not on the relative prioritization of two single output factors, but instead of two institutional logics, represented by three output factors each (as shown in Sections 4.3.3 and 4.3.4. Accordingly, the three virtual weights (unit-invariant, given by the product of an output value and its optimal weight) within each dimension $(w_{DEV1}, w_{DEV2}, w_{DEV3})$ and $(w_{FIN1}, w_{FIN2}, w_{FIN3})$ were added to arrive at two "composite" virtual weights, $w_{DEV}$ and $w_{FIN}$. In the special case of two separate DEA models with a constant dummy input, this "composite" virtual weight essentially equals the respective performance scores resulting from these models. To identify the relative prioritization of the financial logic versus the development logic, the MRT was calculated as the composite virtual weight of the development dimension $(w_{DEV})$ relative to the financial dimension $(w_{FIN})$, whereby a constant of 1 was added to the sum of virtual weights to avoid dividing by a number smaller than 0. The resulting $MRT_{DEV,FIN}$ can range from 0.5 to 1.5,[9] with 1 indicating equal relative importance between the two logics. All points left of 1, that is, between 0.5 and 1, indicate $w_{FIN} > w_{DEV}$, hence a relative prioritization of the financial over the development logic. Contrary, values between 1 and 1.5 indicate a higher relative importance of the development over the financial logic. The $MRT_{DEV,FIN}$, which is subsequently called priority score, reveals MDBs' patterns of relative prioritization of the two institutional logics.

---

[9] Values between 1 and 2 have been rescaled to lie between 1 and 1.5 to make both sides of the scale equally scaled.

**Table 2** Sampled MDBs by type

| Portfolio structure | |
|---|---|
| **Type** | **MDBs** |
| S-MDB | ADB, AfDB, CABEI, CAF, CEDB, IBRD, IDB, IsDB |
| P-MDB | BSTDB, EBRD, EIB,* ICD, IFC, IDB Invest, NIB |
| **Shareholder structure** | |
| **Type** | **MDBs** |
| B-MDB | AfDB, BSTDB, CABEI, CAF, CEDB, EIB, IDB, ICD, IDB Invest, IsDB, NIB |
| C-MDB | ADB, EBRD, IBRD, IFC |

\* Until 2019, the loans extended by the EIB were in the majority to the private sector. In 2019, the EIB has lent predominantly to sovereigns (S&P, 2020, p. 117).

### 4.3.2 Data

For the subsequent analysis, I collected portfolio-level data for a sample of fifteen MDBs, for which consistent lending and capital position data were available. These are the AfDB, ADB, BSTDB, CABEI, CAF, CEDB, EBRD, EIB, IBRD, ICD, IDB, IDB Invest, IFC, IsDB, and NIB. This sample performs very well in terms of representativeness by successfully including both the established and better known MDBs as well as several of the smaller and less known MDBs. Also, it includes several MDBs for each of the types identified in Section 3.4 (S-MDB vs. P-MDB; B-MDB vs. C-MDB), as can be seen in Table 2. This renders possible using this sample to test the hypotheses on the differences across MDB types.[10] Applying a bootstrapping approach minimizes the risk of random noise due to sampling issues and thus additionally helps mitigate potential sampling problems. The period of analysis ranges from 2010 to 2018, so that each MDB has nine observations in the dataset. Thereby, in contrast to cross-sectional data, median performance and priority scores can be calculated for each MDB, reducing the risk of drawing conclusions based on untypical cross-sectional behavior. In total, the data contain 132 observations.[11]

As identified in Section 4.1, the ideal types of the two institutional logics are portfolio composition in ways that maximize allocative performance

---

[10] BDEAC, BOAD, CDB, EADB, EDB, IIB, PIDB, and TDB are excluded for data availability reasons. AIIB, IDA, and NDB are not part of the sample due to their only recent commencement of (debt-financed) operations.

[11] Observations for ICD in 2010 and 2018, and IsDB in 2018 are removed from the dataset due to missing data for all output factors of either dimension.

(development logic) or their capital position and profitability (financial logic). The compliance with institutional demands is measured with three different output factors for each institutional logic.[12] Thanks to DEA's BoD weighting the three output factors can vary in their relative importance across MDBs.

### 4.3.3 Financial Outputs

Based on the measures used in the financial performance literature and in CRA methodologies, the following three indicators for behavior according to the financial logic's demand for capital adequacy are used in the subsequent analysis as financial output measures (see Table 3): MDBs' capital position, profitability, and leverage. MDBs' capital position, first, is measured as equity in relation to assets, and measures "how much capital is available to cover the assets from which risks typically arise" (Moody's, 2019, p. 6).[13] The riskiness of assets (credit risk of borrowers and portfolio concentration) is accounted for by either risk-weighting exposures (as by S&P and Fitch) or using the risk-weight of assets as an ex-post adjustment for the capital position indicator (as by Moody's). The subsequent analysis uses S&P's risk-adjusted capital ratio (RAC ratio), which measures the ratio of equity ("adjusted capital") to risk-weighted assets, adjusted by MDB specificities, such as PCT and portfolio concentration (S&P, 2019, pp. 46–47). Second, MDBs' level of indebtedness, also called leverage, is measured by the debt-to-equity ratio, that is, overall debt burden relative to MDB size. This is relevant since a "large debt stock relative to equity position will imply a lower availability of capital to absorb losses before bondholders are impacted and therefore a higher risk that outstanding debt and debt payments may not be covered" (Moody's, 2017, p. 10). Given that lower rather than higher debt levels are desirable to increase financial performance, MDB debt level is included as the multiplicative inverse of the original output (1/[debt/equity]), which is the most conservative approach to undesirable outputs in DEA (Scheel, 2001, p. 402). Third is profitability, indicating the ability of internal capital generation as a means of strengthening the capital base

---

[12] In DEA, the sample size relative to the number of input and output factors is critical to ensure models have enough discriminating power. The usual sample size requirements, as specified by Sarkis (2007, p. 307) and Huguenin (2012, p. 23), are fully complied with when compliance with each institutional logic is measured with three output factors.

[13] Equity is usually defined as not including callable capital. Instead, callable capital is part of shareholder support assessment (Moody's, 2017, p. 9, 2019, p. 6; Fitch Ratings, 2019, p. 6; S&P, 2018, p. 39). The capital position indicators have different names in the CRA methodologies: 'capital ratio' by S&P (2019) and Fitch Ratings, 2019 or 'asset coverage ratio' by Moody's (2017). Please note that the same indicator is used as its inverse and termed 'leverage' in Moody's (2019). I use the term of the 2017 methodology here to avoid confusion with the indicator for indebtedness.

**Table 3** DEA input and output factors

| Factor | Explanation | Unit |
|---|---|---|
| **Input** | | |
| Constant | Constant single input of 1 for all DMUs | Abs. value |
| **Financial outputs** | | |
| Capital position | Equity/risk-weighted assets (S&P RAC ratio) | x |
| Leverage | Gross debt/equity | % |
| Profitability* | Net income/assets | % |
| **Development outputs** | | |
| Poverty-sensitive lending | Commitments weighted by borrower poverty/total commitments | % |
| Population-sensitive lending | Commitments weighted by borrower population/total commitments | % |
| Policy-sensitive lending | Commitments weighted by borrower policy performance/total commitments | % |

* The ADB recorded a net income in 2017 of USD 31.5 billion, up from 7 million in 2016. This rise is driven mainly by a one-time transfer from the ADF, resulting from the merger of ADB and ADF in 2017 (ADB, 2017, p. 9), which is the number used as numerator for the ADB profitability ratio in 2017.

and thus "to absorb losses and build capital" (Fitch Ratings, 2019, p. 7; see also Moody's, 2019, p. 10; S&P, 2018, p. 38). Recurrent losses, on the other side, "negatively affect capital levels and weaken the ability to absorb shocks" (Moody's, 2019, p. 10). Profitability is a traditional accounting measure and usually measured as returns in relation to assets to account for an organization's relative size.[14]

Data for all three financial output factors were collected from MDB profiles and comparative data tables of several S&P "Supranationals Special Editions" (2015, 2016, 2018, 2019), which provide detailed financial information for multiple MDBs for the five preceding years. In the few instances of inconsistent information across multiple reports, I drew from the respective MDB's annual reports or financial statements. In a few instances, I replaced missing values with zeros, a standard approach in DEA.[15] The effect is that the respective outputs are excluded from the performance evaluation of only those DMUs with missing values. Differently put, DMUs are only evaluated in terms of factors for which data exist. Compared to the traditional approach of list-wise exclusion of DMUs or factors, this method "always yields at least as good an approximation of the ideal frontier based on the full information . . . and possibly a better one" (Kuosmanen, 2009, p. 1769).

### 4.3.4 Development Outputs

Existing efforts to measure donor allocative performance vary across the variables included, the choices of indicators to represent them, and the type of aggregation used (Clist, 2015, p. 819). Yet, there are common factors in the (normative) aid allocation literature to assess allocative performance, which have even entered the (multilateral) development community to determine inter-recipient distributions of concessional funds (cf. Kharas and Noe, 2018).

The "normative principle that aid ought to accrue in priority to the neediest" (Bourguignon and Platteau, 2017, p. 6) is intuitive and usually serves as the main rationale for the provision of aid (McGillivray and Clarke, 2018, p. 1068; White and McGillivray, 1995, p. 165). Aid allocation as an increasing function of recipient need is one of the widely accepted generalizations resulting from the aid allocation literature, based on the argument that aid has a higher development impact in needier countries (Pietschmann, 2014, p. 16) or that it

---

[14] In CRA ratings, asset quality also includes the ratio of impaired or non-performing loans to total loans. However, the share of problem loans is contingent on external conditions so that it is not an ideal indicator for MDBs' adherence to the demands of the financial logic.

[15] Data is missing for all MDBs' 2010 capital positions as well as for the ICD's capital positions of 2011, 2012, 2013. Consequently, data is not missing systematically to a relevant extent for certain MDBs only, reducing the risk of potential bias due to nonrandomly missing data.

equalizes opportunities, based on a Rawlsian theory of justice (Cogneau and Naudet, 2007). In the late 1990s and early 2000s, as part of the broader aid effectiveness discourse, a second rationale became influential: Policy-selectivity of aid,[16] suggesting that aid allocated to recipients with sound policies and high-quality institutional environments can be more effective for economic growth and poverty reduction (Burnside and Dollar, 2004; Collier and Dollar, 2002) or can at the least incentivize recipients to adopt better policies (Guillaumont and Wagner, 2015, p. 22). What follows is that recipient need and institutional quality are commonly considered to be good guidelines for aid allocation (Knack et al., 2011, p. 1908) and are elements of various development agencies' allocation formulas.

As is frequent practice in both the aid allocation literature and many donors' concessional allocation frameworks, need is here conceptualized to include the variables of poverty and population size (in log units to account for their skewed nature). In light of lacking reliable alternatives, poverty is measured in monetary terms as logged income per capita (cf. Birdsall and Kharas, 2010; Knack et al., 2011). The indicators for policy and institutional quality are more contentious, as there is wide disagreement with regard to the underlying concept (Clist, 2015, p. 808). Among them are level of democracy, rule of law, political rights, macroeconomic policy, and corruption (Clist, 2011; Dollar and Levin, 2006; Easterly and Pfutze, 2008; Easterly and Williamson, 2011). The Worldwide Governance Indicators (WGI, Kaufmann et al., 2011) are here used to measure institutional quality, as they integrate several of the aforementioned aspects,[17] have very wide coverage, and are frequently used in (normative) aid allocation research (Birdsall and Kharas, 2010; Roodman, 2012).

In the following analysis, I rely largely on the General Performance Index (GPI, Anderson and Clist, 2011) for measuring allocative performance using the indicators stated in the previous paragraphs. It accommodates all the variables previously identified as relevant (recipient poverty, population, and policy), in the sense that – *ceteris paribus* – a reallocation from a poorer to a richer, larger to smaller, or better to worse governed recipient should worsen the performance measure. In addition, the GPI has several advantages over other allocative performance measurements, and fulfills all of the assessment criteria developed

---

[16] Typically, selectivity is used in the narrow sense of aid being allocated according to the quality of policy and institutional environments of recipients. In a broader sense, selectivity refers to aid allocation along certain criteria that maximize a legitimate objective (Amprou et al., 2007, p. 733). This is the understanding adopted here, with reference to the criteria on which selectivity is based.

[17] Dimensions are voice and accountability, political stability, government effectiveness, regulatory quality, rule of law, and control of corruption.

by White and McGillivray (1995) that are relevant for this study.[18] The GPI is the ratio of the weighted (or discounted) sum of a donor's aid across recipients to that donor's total aid, whereby discounts are mathematically related to recipient desirability. Rather than following the GPI and aggregating the three components (measuring allocation relative to poverty, population, and policy) with arguable weights, I use the three components as separate output factors in DEA, with optimized BoD weights. Hence, equally to the financial output factors in Section 4.3.3, development output factors can vary in their relative importance across MDBs. This leads to the following development output factors:

Population-sensitive lending:

$$\frac{\sum A_{itx} \times \frac{N_{it}-N_{min_t}}{N_{max_t}-N_{min_t}}}{A_{tx}}. \tag{2}$$

Poverty-sensitive lending:

$$\frac{\sum A_{itx} \times \frac{y_{max_t}-y_{it}}{y_{max_t}-y_{min_t}}}{A_{tx}}. \tag{3}$$

Policy-sensitive lending:

$$\frac{\sum A_{itx} \times \frac{G_{it}-G_{min_t}}{G_{max_t}-G_{min_t}}}{A_{tx}}, \tag{4}$$

with $A_{itx}$ being the absolute amount of loans committed to country $i$ by MDB $x$ in year $t$. $N$, $y$, and $G$ are the population, GDP pc (PPP, logged), and WGI score, with the subscript $i$ indicating the respective country and $t$ indicating the year. Subscripts $max$ and $min$ indicate the maximum and minimum of that variable among all those countries which are eligible recipients of that given MDB $x$ in that year $t$ (hence, not only those receiving finance, but all those eligible). $A_{tx}$ is the total sum of commitments of MDB $x$ in year $t$. In simple words, these formulas produce a discounting weight for each eligible country, based on how "desirable" it is relative to the other eligible countries given its level of poverty, population, or institutional quality. This discount is multiplied with the amount of assistance committed to this country in a given year, so that assistance committed to a highly desirable recipient counts more than the same amount committed to a less desirable recipient. Weighted assistance is then summed and related to the

---

[18] See White and McGillivray (1995) and Anderson and Clist (2011) for a discussion of five types of donor allocative performance measures: headcount measures, Suits index, correlation coefficients, regression coefficients, and performance indices.

MDB's total commitments. This results in a measure of how well (from a development perspective) funds are distributed among eligible recipients, ranging from 0 to 1, with a higher number indicating better allocative performance.

I collected an original dataset on the yearly nonconcessional loan commitments in USD millions to each eligible member state for each MDB in the sample, using either the respective country-level information provided in MDBs' annual reports and financial statements or, if no comparable information was available, by aggregating project-level information provided in MDBs' online project databases.[19] Since the argument of this study is made specifically for MDB nonconcessional lending, it was not possible to revert to existing datasets, such as AidData (Tierney et al., 2011), OECD.Stat (OECD, 2021), or AidFlows (World Bank and OECD, 2021). These either do not distinguish between concessional and nonconcessional assistance or include only (mostly concessional) ODA. In addition, existing databases do not have the required wide coverage across various of the smaller MDBs. I extracted the information on the eligibility status of all relevant country-years across all sampled MDBs from numerous MDB reports. For the discounting weights, I collected data on GDP per capita[20] and population size[21] for each country-year from the World Bank's online World Development Indicator database (World Bank, 2019a) and data on institutional quality from the WGI data (World Bank, 2019b).[22]

Table 4 lists descriptive statistics for the six output factors described in Sections 4.3.3 and 4.3.4, three for each logic. It shows that MDBs by no means show uniform behavior across these variables. Instead, across each of these output factors, MDBs have quite substantial variation. Take the example of policy-sensitive lending, which ranges from a low value of 0.23 (CABEI in 2010) to a remarkably high 0.96 (NIB in 2016). On average, MDBs perform best on the population-sensitivity dimension, where the mean value achieved is 0.71, with a minimum value of 0.42, which is much higher than values reached on both the poverty- and the policy-related dimensions. It appears that MDBs pursue different strategic priorities. The question to be explored is whether and how (types of) MDBs differ in the compromise reached between the development and financial logics.

Two DEA specifications are entertained in the subsequent analyses, one for each logic, with three output factors each. For reasons of clarity, the following notation is used, in which the first part refers to the dummy input (always I) and the second part refers to the respective output factor dimension: I-FIN refers to

---

[19] The fiscal year at the World Bank is from July to June. However, as commitment data was taken from IBRD and IFC project databases, it was no difficulty to assign commitments to the respective calendar years.

[20] PPP, based on constant 2011 international \$, as logarithm.      [21] Absolute value, as logarithm.

[22] The six dimensions in the WGI data were aggregated to an additive index with equal weights.

**Table 4** Descriptive statistics of six output factors

| | Variable | Mean | Median | Std. Dev. | Min | Max | N |
|---|---|---|---|---|---|---|---|
| Financial outputs | Profitability | 0.63 | 0.60 | 1.34 | −10.73 | 3.50 | 134 |
| | Leverage (before inverse adjustment) | 3.23 | 2.20 | 2.53 | 0.15 | 9.70 | 134 |
| | Capital position | 26 | 22 | 14.54 | 10 | 92 | 117 |
| Development outputs | Poverty-sensitive lending | 0.42 | 0.41 | 0.13 | 0.16 | 0.70 | 132 |
| | Population-sensitive lending | 0.71 | 0.72 | 0.10 | 0.42 | 0.87 | 132 |
| | Policy-sensitive lending | 0.52 | 0.52 | 0.11 | 0.23 | 0.96 | 132 |

a specification associated with financial performance, with three financial output factors (profitability, capital position, leverage). I-DEV is based on three development output factors (allocation sensitivity to borrower poverty, population, and institutional quality) to measure development performance. For the most parts of the analysis, performance scores are estimated for all MDBs pooled across all years. This way, being estimated relative to one global frontier, performance scores are directly comparable.

## 5 Managing Complexity

The approach outlined in Section 4 results in one score for financial performance per MDB-year and one for development performance per MDB-year. As shown in Table 5, similar to the descriptive statistics of the six output factors in Table 4, MDBs vary considerably in their development and financial performance levels. The variation is smaller for development performance and spread only across the upper half of the possible performance range (the lowest development performance score being 0.60). Financial performance, on the other hand, varies more widely across the sampled MDBs. Mean financial performance is lower and standard deviation larger than for development performance.

### 5.1 Conflicting Institutional Logics

As theorized in Section 3, I expect the development and financial logics to make conflicting demands on MDB development lending. The empirical analysis supports this assumption. Various correlation measures show a statistically significant moderate negative correlation between development and financial performance scores (see Table 6). Since a normal distribution of performance scores cannot necessarily be assumed and is to be rejected according to Shapiro-Wilk tests, nonparametric rank-based measures of association were computed additionally to Pearson's $r$. This indicates that higher compliance with the financial logic tends to lead to lower adherence to the development logic and vice versa.

This is illustrated by the scatterplot in Figure 2, which clearly depicts the negative association between performance scores resulting from I-FIN and I-DEV: The higher an MDB's financial performance (on the $y$-axis), the lower

**Table 5** Descriptive statistics of performance scores

| Performance score | Mean | Median | Std. Dev. | Min | Max |
|---|---|---|---|---|---|
| Development | 0.87 | 0.88 | 0.10 | 0.60 | 0.99 |
| Financial | 0.70 | 0.78 | 0.22 | 0.13 | 0.99 |

**Table 6** Correlation between development and
financial performance scores

| Correlation measure | cor (I-FIN, I-DEV) |
|---|---|
| Pearson's r | −0.44 *** |
| Spearman's rho | −0.42 *** |
| Kendall's tau | −0.30 *** |

*** $p < 0.01$

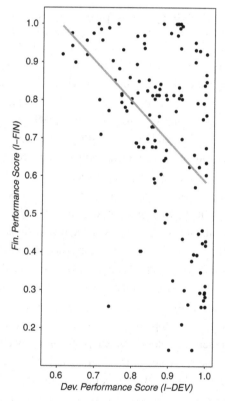

**Figure 2** Scatterplot of performance scores, with trend line

its development performance (on the *x*-axis) tends to be and vice versa. Each of
the corners of the graph represents different MDB behavior. The corner on the
upper left contains MDBs that perform well financially but have poor development performance. In contrast, MDBs in the bottom-right corner show relatively good development performance, but poor financial performance. The
lower-left corner represents relatively low performance on both dimensions.
This part of the graph contains only a single outlier, which indicates that MDBs

in the sample tend to not have both low financial and development performance. In contrast, MDBs in the upper-right corner have relatively high performance on both dimensions. Contrasting to a case of strong incompatibility between the two logics, this corner is not empty. Some MDBs seem to be able to achieve high performance for both logics. Yet, these observations come primarily from the IsDB and ICD, whose high financial performance is a historical contingency, as discussed in more detail in the next section. Excluding IsDB and ICD observations from the correlation analysis results in a Pearson's $r$ of $-0.59$, hence a stronger negative correlation.

## 5.2 Patterns of Prioritization

Based on MDBs' median priority scores, calculated as described in the previous section, MDBs can be arrayed on a continuum spanning from a clear prioritization of the financial logic, which is similar to what would be expected from commercial banks, to a prioritization of the development logic, which is in line with what would normatively be expected from aid agencies (Figure 3): MDBs with a lower median priority score, which are located left to the dashed line indicating equal prioritization of the two logics, emphasize compliance with the demands of the financial over compliance with those of the development logic. In contrast, MDBs on the right side of the continuum have a higher priority score and are thus more similar to aid agencies, prioritizing the development over the financial logic.

The relative prioritization of development and financial institutional demands varies across MDBs. Almost half of the sampled MDBs put larger relative importance on financial over development performance, the other half has opposite priorities. There is additional variation across the MDBs on each side of the continuum: for instance, financial performance is given much stronger emphasis than development performance in the BSTDB compared to the IFC. On the other side, development performance weighs more heavily relative to financial performance at the ADB than CAF. The CEDB, EIB, and NIB clearly stand out due to their unique position on the far right of the continuum. These three European MDBs[23] are located in and lend exclusively to European countries[24] and do not conform to the group-level patterns identified in this section. Therefore, they are subsequently treated as a separate group of MDBs, facing different institutional demands and therefore behaving

---

[23] In the remainder, I use the term 'European MDBs' to refer to these three borrower-dominated B-MDBs that only lend to European countries (CEDB, EIB, NIB). It hence does not pertain to the EBRD, even though it is also active mainly in Europe.

[24] The EIB also lends to countries which are not members of the EU. However, the data analyzed here is restricted to EU member state lending. The same is true for NIB, which occasionally lends to nonmember countries.

**Figure 3** MDBs on a continuum between commercial bank and aid agency

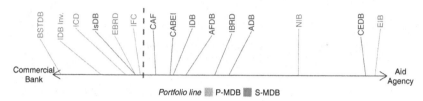

**Figure 4** Continuum by portfolio composition

differently to the others. Therefore, they are largely excluded from the subsequent presentation of results. Instead, they are discussed in more detail in the next section.

The theoretical framework distinguishes MDBs according to portfolio and shareholder composition and expects the resulting MDB types to differ in their relative prioritization of logics, that is, group-level differences between MDBs' priority scores. The first hypothesis expects MDBs that (predominantly or exclusively) lend to the private sector (P-MDBs) to place greater emphasis on the financial than development logic, while those lending to the sovereign sector (S-MDBs) are expected to show the opposite pattern of prioritization. Inspecting the continuum shown in Figure 3 across these two MDB types clearly supports this expectation: Figure 4 shows that all sampled P-MDBs are on the left side of the continuum (excluding the three European MDBs), and hence prioritize financial over development logics, just as expected. In contrast, all S-MDBs except the IsDB are located on the right side of the continuum, indicating that they favor behavior according to development over financial logics. With the exception to the European MDBs (as discussed in the next section), the empirical patterns of relative prioritization across MDBs with different portfolio compositions are in line with what is expected by H1: P-MDBs tend to place greater priority on the financial logic than the development logic, while the compromise found by S-MDBs is in favor of the development logic.

These differences are statistically significant, as shown by two types of one-sided significance tests. Both the Mann–Whitney $U$-test ($U$-test, see Brockett and Golany, 1996) as well as the two-sample Kolmogorov-Smirnov test

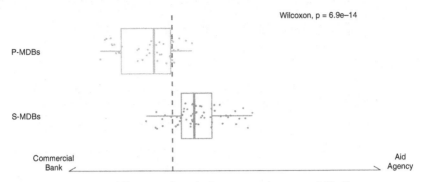

**Figure 5** Differences in priority scores along portfolio lines

(KS test, see Berger and Zhou, 2005) are nonparametric statistical procedures suitable to test whether efficiency scores differ statistically significantly between groups of MDBs. Being nonparametric tests, both are suitable when the exact distribution of efficiency scores is unknown, when the normality assumption is violated as well as for small samples. Its use is thus consistent with the characteristics and goals of DEA. In accordance with Table 4, both the $U$-test and the KS test let us reject the null hypothesis of P-MDBs having the same or higher priority scores at $p < 0.01$.[25] This provides strong evidence that S-MDBs have statistically significantly larger priority scores, that is, place greater priority on the development logic than P-MDBs. This is also illustrated in Figure 5, which plots P-MDBs' and S-MDBs' distributions of priority scores as dots and boxplots.

In addition, the theoretical framework expects borrower-dominated B-MDBs to place greater emphasis on the development logic and nonborrower dominated C-MDBs to prioritize the financial logic. However, results tell a different story (see Figure 6). Differently to what is expected by the second hypothesis, MDBs of both types are found on both sides of the continuum. As such, sampled C-MDBs are at the rightmost end of each of the continuum's two sides, while B-MDBs tend to populate the two left ends. This again does not include the three European MDBs, which are discussed in Section 6.3.

Accordingly, the respective $U$-tests and KS tests do not let us reject the null hypothesis that B-MDBs have higher priority scores, that is, place greater emphasis on the development logic compared to C-MDBs. Differently to original expectations, B-MDBs tend to place higher priority (instead of lower) on the financial logic than C-MDBs. However, the emerging pattern is less clear-cut than for the differentiation along portfolio lines.

---

[25] The test statistic of the $U$-test is $U = 2,438$ and that of the KS test is $D^- = 0.78$. These tests exclude the three European MDBs.

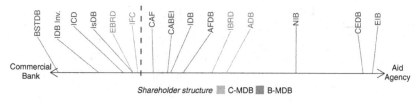

Shareholder structure ■ C-MDB ■ B-MDB

**Figure 6** Continuum by shareholder structure

## 5.3 A New MDB Typology

Together, the results of Section 5.2 suggest explanatory value to both dimensions of portfolio and shareholder composition combined: Portfolio structure determines MDBs' location on the left or right side of the continuum, while their relative position on that side is driven by shareholder composition. For this reason, the following section goes beyond the expectations made in the theoretical framework and explores the value of constructing a new 2 × 2 typology, as shown in Table 7.

This typology is valuable only if it describes distinct groups regarding MDB compliance with and prioritization of the two institutional logics. To assess whether this is the case, I start with a visual inspection of performance score data. The scatterplot in Figure 7 is the same as previously shown in Figure 2, this time with observations colored by MDB type. As can be seen, the new 2 × 2 typology describes distinct patterns of prioritization, given the high levels of intra-group consistency and inter-group difference across types (the four larger triangles indicate averages per type, excluding European and Islamic MDBs). As previously stated, the European MDBs (nonsolid diamond shapes at the lower right side) as well as the Islamic MDBs (IsDB and ICD, nonsolid diamond shapes in the upper-right corner) deviate from the other MDBs, forming their own groups, as set forth in Section 6.3.

In addition to pairwise $U$-tests and KS tests, a global Kruskal–Wallis rank sum test was used to check the statistical significance of the above differences. Testing group-wise differences in development and financial performance scores, respectively, consistently shows that the four types of MDBs are significantly different in their levels of development and financial performance. All results are statistically significant at the 1 percent level, with the only exception of one pairwise comparison (type II vs. IV on the development dimension), which is significant at the 5 percent level.[26] For reasons of scope, the test statistics and levels of significance for all pairwise and global tests conducted are not presented here.

---

[26] These tests excluded the three European MDBs and the two Islamic MDBs for the reasons stated in Section 6.3.

**Table 7** A new 2 × 2 typology of MDBs

|  |  | Portfolio structure | |
|  |  | Sovereign-lending (S-MDB) | Private-lending (P-MDB) |
| --- | --- | --- | --- |
| Shareholder structure | Creditor-dominated (C-MDB) | *I (S/C-MDB)* ADB, IBRD | *II (P/C-MDB)* EBRD, IFC |
|  | Borrower-dominated (B-MDB) | *III (S/B-MDB)* AfDB, CABEI, CAF, CEDB, IDB, IsDB | *IV (P/B-MDB)* BSTDB, EIB, ICD, IDB Invest, NIB |

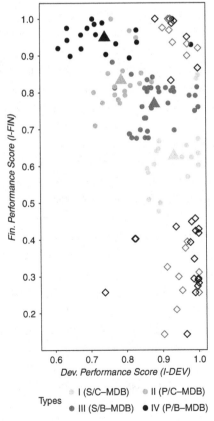

**Figure 7** Development and financial performance scores by MDB type

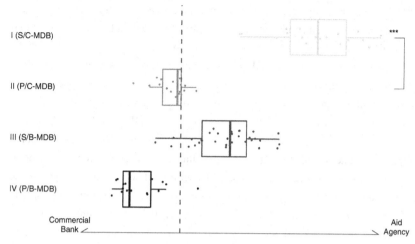

**Figure 8** Significant group differences: Priority scores
*** $p < 0.01$

Significance tests on the differences in the relative prioritization of the development and financial logics across types also reveal significantly different priority patterns across the four MDB types, as visualized in Figure 8. The plot shows for each MDB type the distribution of priority scores as dots and boxplots. On the right side are horizontal bars indicating the level of significance of some pairwise comparisons using *U*-tests. Of all sovereign-lending S-MDBs, which tend to prioritize the development over the financial logic, the creditor-dominated S/C-MDBs (type I) put a relatively larger emphasis on the development logic than borrower-dominated S/B-MDBs (type III). The analysis also suggests that the private-lending P-MDBs (types II and IV) are mostly located on the left side of the dashed equality line, and hence prioritize the financial logic. Among the P-MDBs, it is the borrower-dominated P/B-MDBs (type IV) which have a relatively stronger prioritization of the financial logic compared to creditor-dominated P/C-MDBs (type II).

The statistical tests show that the four MDB types of this new 2 × 2 typology indeed constitute four statistically distinct groups that show significant differences in their compliance with the two institutional logics. Also, they have significantly different priorities when compromising between the two logics as a response to institutional complexity. Thereby, portfolio line tends to determine the side of the continuum between commercial bank and aid agency on which MDBs are located. S-MDBs with a sovereign-lending portfolio are closer to aid agencies, while P-MDBs lending to the private sector are located closer to commercial banks. Shareholder structure affects MDBs' relative positions on a given side of the continuum: Keeping portfolio structure constant, C-MDBs in which nonborrowing creditor members have the majority of votes place a stronger relative emphasis on the development logic than borrower-dominated B-MDBs, which more strongly prioritize the financial logic.

In addition to evaluating MDB performance and priorities relative to a pooled frontier (i.e. simultaneously including MDBs of all four types), I conducted supplementary analyses into the sources of group-wise differences. While intragroup performance differences stem from MDB-specific management decisions, intergroup differences are caused by varying operating conditions, such as production technologies, geographic locations, resource endowment, capacities, policies and regulations, and operational setting, and represent the gap between operating conditions available to all DMUs and those faced by a group of DMUs (Walheer, 2018). Methods available for disentangling idiosyncratic (group internal) performance differences from inter-group systematic heterogeneity can be categorized into metafrontier- and Malmquist index-based approaches (Asmild, 2015; O'Donnell et al., 2008). For this analysis, both the Global frontier difference index, which is a Malmquist-based approach (Asmild, 2015) and metatechnology ratios (O'Donnell et al., 2008) were calculated. For reasons of conciseness, in the following, I do not in detail report the methods and findings of this analysis but instead focus on the main results.

Combining the results of the group-specific frontiers with those of the pooled frontier leads to interesting conclusions: As shown in Figures 7 and 8, the four MDB types perform differently regarding both the development and the financial logic and hence show significantly different patterns of prioritization. The additional group-specific frontier analysis reveals that the four types have significantly different best practice frontiers, which implies that performance differences between them are due to systematic heterogeneity. This means that the four MDB types face systematically different restrictions and opportunities, determining the performance limits for all MDBs of a given type. Take as an example the development performance differences between types I and IV. The analysis based on a pooled frontier shows that, on average, type I MDBs outperform type IV MDBs. Additional analyses now show that this difference is systematic: Given the different opportunity sets of the two types of MDBs, not even the best performing MDBs of type IV reach a level of development performance that gets close to the group-specific best practice frontier of type I MDBs. These findings grant additional support to the new 2 × 2 MDB typology and demonstrate its usefulness for understanding MDB lending operations. The resulting four types of MDBs vary statistically significantly in their development and financial performance, and consequently in their compromising patterns in response to institutional complexity. Interestingly, these differences stem from systematic disparities in restrictions and opportunities.

## 5.4 Robustness Checks

I conducted several robustness checks. As previously stated, estimates are bias-corrected via bootstrapping to reduce random noise (Simar and Wilson, 1998). Several additional DEA models have been estimated, based on either modified operationalizations of the output factors or on different model specifications. Moreover, I estimated pooled time series linear regression models with the shareholder and portfolio compositions as the independent variables and a "simple" additive index of the standardized components of the development and financial logics, respectively, as dependent variables. The results of all additional models are very much in line with those of the main models, increasing robustness of the results presented in Sections 5.1, 5.2, and 5.3.

First, instead of the operationalization of the three development output factors with total MDB commitments in the denominator, as described in the previous section, I also constructed them as a ratio of weighted commitments to equity. This measure captures not only the quality of the allocation of available sums but also the total amount made available relative to an MDB's size. It therefore is a stricter evaluation standard, resulting in an even stronger negative correlation between development and financial performance. However, correlating financial and development performance using this alternative measure runs the risk of a spurious correlation, given that equity is a common denominator to some of the output factors on both sides of the correlation. For this reason, the main analysis relies on the development output factors as described in the previous section, which is a more conservative measurement approach. Also, I used an alternative measure of capital position, namely the unweighted equity-to-assets ratio, which is available for all years of the study period and does not include S&P's risk-weights and MDB-specific adjustments, which could entail biases. The resulting financial performance scores are highly robust to this change. I chose to use the RAC ratio in the main analysis, as it does incorporate additional relevant aspects such as portfolio concentration and riskiness of assets, which are relevant in the financial logic.

A second set of robustness checks is not applying BoD weighting to make sure that results are not driven by my methodological approach. Instead, two equally weighted additive indices of development and financial performance are formed by the three standardized output factors associated with each institutional logic. As can be expected, MDBs reach lower performance scores in this specification, as they are no longer granted the benefit of the doubt. Nevertheless, results of this specification are very similar to the main specification using BoD weighting. Performance scores are highly correlated across the two specifications (correlation between the development performance scores of the main and this specification is 0.9, that between the financial performance scores is 0.88). The negative association between the two institutional logics is stronger in this than in the main DEA analysis, indicating that the BoD-weighted performance scores are more conservative measures for compliance with the two logics and their relative prioritization across MDBs. Pooled time-series linear regression models of the binary indicators of portfolio and shareholder composition show a statistically significant positive effect ($p < 0.1$) of portfolio composition on the "simple" additive development index and no effect on the financial additive index. Shareholder composition has, as indicated by the main results, no significant effect on both "simple" indices. When adding an interaction term of shareholder and portfolio composition, both main effects and the interaction term are statistically significant ($p < 0.01$) on the "simple" development and the "simple" financial performance indices. This gives additional support to the value of the proposed $2 \times 2$ typology.

Finally, the observations of the three European (CEBD, EIB, NIB) and the two Islamic MDBs (ICD, IsDB) have been excluded from the estimation of the best practice frontiers to ensure that results are not driven by the inclusion of these MDBs, which show exceptional, deviant behavior compared to the other MDBs. The negative association between the two logics and the distribution of performance scores are robust to the exclusion of these five MDBs.

## 6 Discussion

Insights I have gained in semistructured expert interviews with key informants (including officials of the financial risk units at the IBRD, IDB, and IFC, [senior advisors to] Executive Directors [ED] of borrowing and nonborrowing countries at these MDBs, and a CRA credit analyst) corroborate and help to contextualize the stated arguments and empirical findings on the conflicting dual nature of MDBs as well as their responses thereto.

### 6.1 Relevance of the Two Institutional Logics

Certainly, both logics – the development and the financial logic – play important roles in MDB development lending. Next to their acknowledgement of the MDBs' development mandates, interview partners repeatedly emphasized MDBs' reliance on capital markets and consequently the importance of the financial logic. The AAA rating – at least at the World Bank Group and IDB – is nonnegotiable to shareholders. It is a "central, a crucial component" (interview with World Bank risk management director, June 3, 2019) and "one of the key objectives" (interview with World Bank senior credit risk manager,

May 17, 2019), as it allows MDBs to borrow from markets at very low rates (interview with risk management officials at the World Bank, June 3, 2019, July 1, 2019).

A senior advisor to a World Bank ED noted: "You can agree or not with credit rating agencies, but they are there, so you have to deal with them if you want to access the market" (interview at the World Bank, July 3, 2019). Therefore, one of the ED advisors at the World Bank even described CRAs as "quasi regulators" (interview, May 20, 2019) and a financial expert consulting several of the smaller MDBs spoke of the "draconian influence" of CRAs (interview, September 27, 2019). Both IBRD and IDB maintain an active dialogue and regular meetings with the "Big Three". In their internal credit risk models, the IBRD tries to replicate CRA models to project what is required to secure a AAA rating (interview with a high-ranking IBRD risk manager, June 3, 2019), being even "a bit more conservative than the rating agencies" (interview with an IFC risk manager, June 19, 2019).

The importance of the financial logic is also based on the informality of the PCT, which does not make it fully reliable. When a country's debt is mostly multilateral, PCT cannot be taken for granted. Increased collateralized lending, for example by China, additionally dilutes PCT, as it puts multilateral debt second in cases of payment difficulties (interviews at the World Bank, May 17, 2019, June 4, 2019, July 1, 2019). As expected, shareholders therefore demand MDB financial performance to avoid a capital call, which would "peg their budgets" (interview with senior advisor to a World Bank ED, June 4, 2019).

As assumed, empirical results show that the two institutional logics are conflicting, given that the higher the financial performance of MDBs, the lower their development performance tends to be and vice versa. There is a trade-off between the two logics and MDBs need to navigate the volatile institutional complexity this evokes. Although both logics are inherently built into the MDB business model, the extent of capital market financing and consequently the efforts spent on financial concerns as well as the extent to which the financial logic would impact compliance with the development logic were originally not foreseen (cf. Humphrey, 2016b, p. 93, 2017a, p. 300; Mohammed, 2004, p. 15).

Several of my interviewees confirmed this trade-off. There is, first, the question of overall business volume, which MDBs would want to increase for more development impact, as a unit chief at the IDB Risk Department explained. However, this is prohibited by the financial logic and its financial viability demands (interview, July 18, 2019). Second, the trade-off materializes in portfolio riskiness, which senior risk managers at the IDB and IBRD described as a zero-sum game. Increased portfolio riskiness entails a business volume reduction given the board's capital adequacy requirements, whereas a higher overall lending volume requires a lower level of riskiness. Capital held back in reserves, however, is not available for other development operations (interviews, May 29 and July 1, 2019). Similarly, a AAA rating requires a relatively larger capital cushion than AA. MDBs need to weigh the benefits of having AAA, such as lower borrowing costs, against the additional usable capital freed by an AA rating, as a World Bank ED advisor stressed (interview, May 20, 2019). Conflicting demands also become visible in loan sizes. An IFC financial risk expert noted that in the development logic, MDBs need to make numerous relatively small investments, as those most in need of capital usually cannot afford larger loans. This, however, is unpopular within the financial logic, as the cost of doing business relative to the volume of business is much higher in this case, which is detrimental to profits (interview with IFC risk manager, June 19, 2019).

Just as institutional complexity theory expects, the resulting operational context is challenging to MDBs. "One of the biggest differences is that commercial banks would never lend to all of our clients" as a World Bank credit risk analyst stressed (interview, July 1, 2019). "We have a very high-risk business portfolio and at the same time our risk appetite and the Board's risk appetite have remained at maintaining a AAA rating", as an IFC strategic risk department official stressed (interview, June 19, 2019). One of his colleagues added that MDBs' choices to improve credit quality are much more restrained than in commercial banks due to the development mandate. While commercial banks are willing to take certain risks if they are balanced by sufficient returns, MDBs must take on risks in return for development impact (interview with World Bank senior risk manager, May 17, 2019).

## 6.2 Compromising between Conflicting Logics

Based on the characteristics of the institutional complexity present in multilateral development banking, MDBs need to craft a compromise between the two logics at play, which is a "key strategic discussion", as an IFC risk manager has stated (interview, June 19, 2019). Accordingly, several of my interview partners described that the solution to the trade-off MDBs face is "to prioritize. . . . It is a balancing act" (interview with IDB risk management unit chief, July 18, 2019). MDBs need to "get a balance between delivering the mission of the bank and doing it in a financially sustainable way" (interview with World Bank ED senior advisor, June 4, 2019) or, in other words, "the goal is to make sure that we are lending out as much money as we can to places that can use it and need it the most, while ensuring the financial sustainability of the World Bank itself" (interview with World Bank credit risk analyst, July 1, 2019). "You have to balance the risk to the financial soundness of the bank with its role as a development lender. . . . That is why balance is important. Always weighing the risk and the relevant impact. And that is a fine line" (interview with World Bank senior credit risk manager, May 17, 2019). Only when MDBs do sound risk management to be financially sustainable can they uphold their development operation: "it does not do anyone good if the institution cannot make any more loans" (interview with World Bank credit risk analyst, July 1, 2019). Yet, excessive financial performance could challenge the very necessity of a public organization (Woods, 2006, p. 9). In the words of an IDB risk management unit chief, "if you are not relevant to your members, you disappear. If you cannot sustain financially, you disappear" (interview, July 18, 2019).

The results of the quantitative analysis show that, based on the relative prioritization of the two logics, MDBs hold separate locations on a continuum between commercial bank and aid agency behavior. Notably, the observed variance aligns with coherent types. In line with the first hypothesis, MDBs which lend only or primarily to the private sector clearly place stronger emphasis on the financial over the development logic than MDBs that lend to sovereigns. One reason are stricter demands by capital markets faced by P-MDBs. Lending to the private sector, P-MDBs do not benefit from PCT and usually have no callable capital to serve as guarantee. Also, P-MDBs extend loans to more diverse and numerous sets of borrowers, making risk analysis more demanding but crucial. As an IFC risk manager stated, for these reasons P-MDBs "have to be extremely prudent in how we manage our financial risks" (interview, June 19, 2019). P-MDBs are "exposed to the same risks as commercial banks", with the consequence that risk management is more "complex" at P-MDBs compared to S-MDBs (interview with World Bank ED advisor, May 20, 2019).

For example, at S&P, which has the most quantitative and formulaic, but also most restrictive approach among the "Big Three" (Humphrey, 2017a, p. 287) and was mentioned in expert interviews to be the most relevant to MDBs, S-MDBs regularly receive upgrades for their PCT and highly rated callable capital. In contrast, P-MDBs do not enjoy these uplifts but instead face the risk of being penalized for their relatively lower portfolio performances. To secure high credit ratings, which they depend on nevertheless, P-MDBs need to devote a more serious financial effort than S-MDBs. Accordingly, "credit officers . . . at the IFC are some of the most senior and highly respected people in the corporation" (interview with IFC risk manager, June 19, 2019). IFC has "an extremely strong risk department" with a "solid power base", having a notable number of touch points during the project cycle, which it uses to gradually adjusts loan conditions in line with a prudent risk approach at the expense of what might be expedient from a development impact perspective (interview with World Bank ED advisor, May 20, 2019). P-MDBs can afford to do so as they usually hold a much less prominent position on the public agenda and are hence less publicly scrutinized. For example, the IFC is less "high-profile" and "less symbolic" than the IBRD (interview with IFC risk manager, June 19, 2019).

While empirical results are in line with what was theoretically expected, they do not show a complete sorting according to portfolio composition. Instead, results indicate that keeping portfolio structure constant, shareholder composition plays a role for which logic MDBs prioritize. This confirms both the argument's falsifiability and the variability among the MDBs. Differently to what H2 expected, borrower-dominated B-MDBs place a stronger relative emphasis on the financial logic than C-MDBs. One of the likely reasons is yet again that B-MDBs feel exposed to more demanding pressures by CRAs, urging them to compensate for an a priori lack of legitimacy they suffer (cf. Pache and Santos, 2013, pp. 993–994): B-MDBs usually have lower shares of highly rated callable capital at their disposal and therefore less frequently get the respective rating upgrades than C-MDBs. Quite the opposite, B-MDBs face the risk of being penalized by S&P for borrowing member states having "a significant influence over decision-making" (S&P, 2020, 54). As has been explained by a S&P credit analysts responsible for MDB ratings, B-MDBs could have an "incentive structure that is set up to support the possibility that decisions will be made to maximize [borrowing members'] return over the capital position", which "from a credit perspective is one factor that we look at on the governance side in terms of capturing potential agency risk" (interview with S&P director, July 16, 2019). An example of this risk materializing is CAF's continued lending to Venezuela in past years, despite the high financial risks involved. Being a B-MDB, one explanation for this could be that the other borrowing shareholders are not inclined to stop lending, for fear of losing out were they ever in a comparable situation (interview with IDB risk management unit chief, May 29, 2019, July 18, 2019). Similarly, borrowers at the World Bank usually try to minimize criticism toward other countries' projects to not be neglected themselves in future lending (interview with World Bank ED advisor, May 20, 2019). As a consequence of these B-MDB-specific penalization risks, B-MDBs might (feel the) need to show higher financial performance than C-MDBs in order to fulfill CRAs' requirements (cf. Delikanli et al., 2018, p. 37), resulting in their observed higher relative prioritization of the financial logic. One additional mechanism might be at work here. Compared to B-MDBs, C-MDB are mostly larger, more prestigious, and more established, with internationally more powerful shareholders. This could result in more opportunities to cultivate regular and close contact with CRAs. Thereby, C-MDBs might know better about the level of financial performance required for a desired rating and might be able to better reassure CRAs of their good financial standing.

Summing up, results suggest that in addition to the shareholder dimension, which has been used as a categorizing variable in previous research (Birdsall, 2018; Humphrey, 2014), portfolio structure can help shed additional light on MDB behavior. The resulting 2 × 2 typology describes four types of MDBs with significantly different strategic behavior.

## 6.3 Exceptional MDB Behavior

As stated in Section 5, some MDBs' responses to institutional complexity deviate from the majority of MDBs, which I call the "conventional" MDBs here. In what follows, these other MDBs are discussed in more detail to explain their deviant behavior.

### 6.3.1 The European MDBs

The three European MDBs (CEDB, EIB, NIB) are found in the empirical analysis to have a considerably lower financial and higher development performance than the "conventional" MDBs, which places them on the far right of the continuum. A closer look reveals that results stem from differing demands made on the European and the "conventional" MDBs by the two logics, which for the European MDBs limits the comparability and validity of the indicators used in this study.

The European MDBs' low financial performance, as measured here, is a result of their least conservative capital positions and by far highest debt-to-equity ratios of all MDBs in the sample. Yet, this does not actually indicate a disregard for markets' demands: despite their seemingly unfavorable financial performance on the chosen financial output factors, all three European MDBs are most highly rated by CRAs. Instead, CRAs – according to their own reports – do not see a major concern in the high leverage and low capital cushions of these three MDBs, mainly because of their much wealthier and further "developed" shareholder and borrower base. CRAs regularly reward European MDB port-folios' high performance and low risk classes, given that most shareholders have top credit ratings themselves. Also, while S&P assigns a penalty for being borrower-dominated to MDBs like the AfDB, CDB, IsDB, or NDB (S&P, 2020, pp. 70, 88, 157, 160), this does not come into effect for CEDB, EIB, and NIB. In addition, CRAs appreciate that both CEDB and NIB benefit from PCT even in their private sector lending and that the EIB benefits from European Commission guarantees for many of its loans.

Hence, while CRAs, as intermediate signalers of financial risks and prime institutional referents of the financial logic, request low leverage and high capital adequacy of the "conventional" MDBs, their demands seem to considerably differ for the three European MDBs. Accordingly, these can afford relatively high leverage and comparably low capital adequacy (translating into low financial performance as measured here), without risking top credit ratings. This is in line with the observation made by Kapur and Raychaudhuri (2014, p. 7), according to which CRAs look at the European MDBs differently.[27] This coincides with the institutional logics literature, which states that high-status organizations often enjoy high legitimacy, allowing them to partly liberate themselves from institutional pressures (Battilana et al., 2017, p. 142; Pache and Santos, 2013, p. 994).

Similarly, the development demands made on the three European MDBs are different to those on the "conventional" MDBs in several ways. Given the specific historical contexts at their creation and the fact that the European member states mostly have more advanced economies, the purpose of these MDBs is less focused on traditional economic development and instead more on social and economic integration and cooperation (e.g. CEDB, 2021; Clifton et al., 2018, pp. 735–737). These different demands, however, are not captured by indicators derived from the aid allocation literature (which deals with less "developed" countries). The indicators used in this study to measure development performance hence lose their validity when it comes to MDBs serving advanced economies. This implies that the results of the European MDBs are comparable to those of the "conventional" MDBs only to a limited extend. Instead, respective financial and development performance levels need to be assessed in future studies using alternative indicators.

### 6.3.2 The Islamic MDBs

The second set of exceptional observations are of the two MDBs in the sample that operate in accordance with the principles of Sharia: IsDB and its private sector arm, ICD. They provide religiously acceptable financial services to Muslim communities, which, in contrast to Western banking, prohibits the payment and receipt of interest in all forms (Hassan and Lewis, 2007, pp. 1–2). Both IsDB and ICD extend financial assistance via Sharia-compliant

---

[27] Kapur and Raychaudhuri (2014, p. 7) count the EBRD to the European MDBs. This contrasts the results of this book, in which relative performance at the EBRD is in line with that of the 'conventional' MDBs. This makes sense considering that since the time of Kapur and Raychaudhuri's (2014) article, the EBRD has increasingly expanded its operations into non-European and financially more risky countries, such as the MENA region.

instruments, among them interest-free loans, equity participation, leasing, and profit sharing (Ray and Kamal, 2019, p. 206). For both MDBs, the empirical analysis remarkably finds high development and financial performance at the same time, even though the theoretical framework expects a conflicting relationship between the two institutional logics. The findings for the two Islamic MDBs could hence disprove the theoretical argument and provide insights into how MDBs can adhere to the demands of both logics. However, these exceptional findings are due to a peculiarity in the IsDB's and ICD's operational history and trail off at closer inspection.

These MDBs' high financial performance scores are driven primarily by their extremely low leverage compared to peers, which is a consequence of operations at the two Islamic MDBs having initially been funded exclusively through members' equity. Only since 2003 are resources raised directly from markets via Sharia-compliant instruments (IsDB, 2013, p. 21). This explains their still low debt-to-equity ratios. Accordingly, the IsDB's and ICD's development performance is high when measured in terms of assistance weighted by borrowers' desirability relative to total assistance. Yet, when assessing development performance via allocation relative to equity, their performance scores deteriorate sharply. Using the former measure (as done in the main results presented in the previous section), mean development performance of both the IsDB and ICD stands at 94 percent. In contrast, when relating the weighted allocations to equity, values drop to 27 percent for the IsDB and 12 percent for the ICD, which is among the developmentally worst performing MDBs of the sample. While the change in the denominator of the development output factors does not make a major difference for most other MDBs, it has a very large impact on the IsDB and ICD. The reason again lies in their extremely low leverage. This implies that the two Islamic MDBs are not directly comparable to the other MDBs on the measurements for logic compliance used in this analysis, as they reach high levels of financial and development performance mainly due to their historically founded low leverage.

## 6.4 Scope and Limitations of Study

As in every research, despite careful considerations, some limitations remain. Given its research design, this analysis can neither establish causal effects nor disentangle different explanations for observed MDB behavior. Institutional logics influence organizational behavior through shaping actors' identities and goals (Thornton et al., 2012, pp. 85–89). While the theoretical argument and interpretation of results focus on the latter, the methodological approach does not disentangle the micro-level causal mechanisms at play. For reasons of comparability, MDBs are treated in this research as unitary actors and institutional demands as well as responses taken are considered only on the organizational level. This approach is useful for a comparison of several MDBs, but it comes at the cost of neglecting the role of MDB subunits and of individual-level interests, norms, and socializations in enacting institutional demands. Only a detailed qualitative study could trace micro-level causal mechanisms. However, in my understanding, this lack of a clear distinction between the causal mechanisms linking institutional logics to action is a common flaw in much of the institutional logics literature. The relatively comprehensive understanding of institutional logics guiding action via shaping identities, cognition, and goals makes it difficult to disentangle causal mechanisms, both theoretically and empirically (on this point, see also Wry et al., 2013).

Despite not testing causal mechanisms, the results of the quantitative analysis prove to be robust across different specifications and gain validity from being in line with theoretical expectations and statements by several experts. Thereby, the relatively large and heterogeneous sample of MDBs included in this study increases the generalizability of findings and the arguments and results claim validity beyond the MDBs on which the analysis is based. Yet, similar to Humphrey (2019), future research could validate the identified demands and patterns of compromise for the MDBs excluded from the sample, which are primarily small B-MDBs from the Global South. Additionally, the dual nature of singular MDBs, where voting shares of borrowers changed to exceed/fall below 50 percent, could be explored with the help of quasi-experimental analysis.

The operationalization of development and financial performance determines the scope of drawable conclusions. Importantly, the argument is made and tested for nonconcessional MDB operations only. It hence does not necessarily apply equally to concessional lending arms or trust funds administered by MDBs. Financial performance is operationalized in terms of the most important demands made by the international investment community. This approach is stretched to its limits for the European MDBs, where it seems that CRAs apply slightly different rating standards. Therefore, the indicators used here to measure financial performance cannot lead to comparable results across the European/non-European MDB divide. On the other side, since development itself is a complicated and dynamic concept, as there are multiple possible definitions and disagreements about what it requires (Babb, 2009, p. 1), the measurement of development performance is very complex. There is a plethora of demands made by the development logic, extending to relatively new topics such as climate change, migration, income inequality, and global public goods (cf. Kodera, 2017, p. 11). In this study, I have clearly limited the operationalization of development performance to allocative performance, that is, the geographical distribution of nonconcessional MDB assistance.

It is important to stress, again, that allocative performance does not directly measure development impact, since aid process performance is a necessary but not sufficient condition for achieving favorable outcomes (Gutner and Thompson, 2010, p. 236). This choice was made to allow for a clear comparative assessment across MDBs for one area of development logic demands with relatively clear normative guidelines, where data are collectable, comparable, and analyzable across several MDBs. Yet, this way, the empirical analysis adopts a supply-side perspective, disregarding whether countries would even want to borrow from an MDB (Humphrey and Michaelowa, 2013, p. 143) and does not take into account whether borrowers have the absorptive capacity to implement the projects. This approach excludes from the empirical analysis other relevant aspects of the development logic, which are either difficult to measure empirically; where it is not entirely clear how they should be configured to contribute to development; or where it would be very difficult to integrate them all concisely into one model, partly because they pertain to different operational levels. Also, as stated in Section 6.3.1, the used indicators for development performance lose validity in the case of the European MDBs. Future efforts to include additional aspects of the development logic could rely on development impact assessment scores, as increasingly conducted by MDBs themselves. These include the "Results and Performance" database of the World Bank Group (2020), the ADB "Results Framework" (ADB, 2020a), or the IFC's "Anticipated Impact Measurement and Monitoring" (IFC, n.d.), the data of which are, however, not necessarily comparable across MDBs. These scores are not comparable and available across a larger number of MDBs, and therefore were not suitable measurements for the present study. But they might prove useful for future single-case studies or as a basis to develop more comprehensive measurements of development logic compliance.

Finally, this study is limited to two institutional logics, leaving aside the issue of shareholder political influence, which has been shown to be an important driver of MDB behavior (e.g. Babb, 2009). Yet, this variable is "muted" here, given that the institutional complexity formed by the development and the financial logics provides the institutional environment for shareholder political interference. As the renowned World Bank expert Devesh Kapur and his colleague have stated, the existence of the financial logic provides "an external discipline that mitigate[s] the politicization" of MDBs by their owners (Kapur and Raychaudhuri, 2014, p. 2). This is in line with Tamar Gutner's argument that the most important variable to understand MDB behavior is how much relative strength it grants to the development and financial logics, while "[d]onor preferences ... are not sufficient in determining which activities and projects a bank is willing and able to offer recipient countries" (2002, p. 75).

## 7 Conclusion

In the course of the 2018 World Bank capital increase, member state capital injection was tied to expanded IFC operations in fragile and conflict-affected states (FCAS) (Edwards, 2018). Simultaneously, IDA issued its first ever bond, marking its debut in private market capital raising (World Bank, 2018).[28] Thereupon, based on the resulting heightened relevance of the financial logic at IDA, observers cautioned of higher interest rates of IDA lending and consequently increased debt crisis risk among borrowers (Bretton Woods Project, 2017). On a related note, the already well-established financial logic at the IFC is feared to lead to a "push [into] big, easy, low-impact, low-additionality projects" (Kenny et al., 2018) in FCAS. Relatedly, MDBs' current push into private sector operations as well as into the mobilization of private finance could entail a growing importance of the financial logic, potentially at the expense of the development logic (cf. Jomo and Chowdhury, 2019; Stein and Sridhar, 2017). The implication is that private sector mobilization is not the right tool for all types of sectors and projects (cf. Kapoor, 2019).

These recent developments in the MDB system exemplify and stress the importance of a fuller understandings of the dual nature of the MDBs. This Element does precisely that: It shows the complex relationship between the development and financial natures of MDBs. It helps to gain a deeper understanding of ongoing processes, pressures, and limits of multilateral development banking, which is central for the appropriate design and evaluation of MDB operations. This Element is among the first to highlight the relevance of financial considerations in MDB operations and the first to conceptualize and illustrate how these are related to the attainment of MDBs' mandated development objectives. Different to previous MDB research, this study places the dual nature of MDBs at its center and develops an argument that extends to the entire MDB universe. It systematically compares the relative importance granted to MDBs' financial versus development goals across MDBs, based on a carefully derived set of indicators and a newly assembled dataset of financial indicators and the geographical allocation of nonconcessional loans across eligible borrowers at fifteen MDBs from 2010 to 2008. Based on the prioritization of development versus financial demands, this Element locates MDBs on a continuum between

---

[28] IDA used to be fully funded by member state contributions and is partly debt-financed only since 2018. Therefore, it is not part of the empirical analysis, although it now qualifies as MDB according to the definition developed in this book.

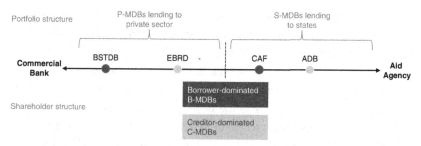

**Figure 9** Types of MDBs on a continuum between commercial
bank and aid agency

**Source**: Author's figure.

commercial bank and aid agency (see Figure 9). It explores variance in MDBs' response patterns to institutional complexity, showing statistically significantly different responses across the types of a newly developed 2 × 2 typology. Private-lending, borrower dominated P/B-MDBs (such as the BSTDB) have the strongest prioritization for the financial logic, at the largest expense of compliance with the development logic's demands. This is similar but less strong for private-lending, creditor dominated P/C-MDBs (such as the EBRD). On the other side of the continuum, sovereign-lending, creditor-dominated S/C-MDBs (such as the ADB) place the strongest priority on compliance with the development logic. This is similar for sovereign-lending, borrower-dominated S/B-MDBs (like CAF), which show a less extreme development logic prioritization.

Throughout, this study illustrates the applicability and value of the institutional logics perspective to MDB and broader IO research. This theoretical framework provides us with an explicit and well-grounded analytical lens to acknowledge the existence of multiple logics guiding IO behavior and can draw attention to the challenges arising thereof. Thereby, it offers a conceptual language to analyze a variety of topics. In combination with this theoretical foundation, DEA can serve as a suitable tool for systematically and comparatively assessing IO behavior. They can also be transferred to other contexts in the fields of development economics and IR. One is that of national development banks, which in many ways resemble the business model of MDBs and have more recently experienced a push on the international development agenda (Griffith-Jones, 2016). The current paradigm shift in the response to refugee crises toward increased cooperation between humanitarian and development actors (cf. Zetter, 2021) is another example of how the institutional complexity framework could be applied to an issue in IR and development economics.

Thanks to their unique business model, MDBs have been outstanding in leveraging their resources to make funds available to contexts that are not sufficiently served by private capital markets. Despite – or, in ways more accurately, because of – their powerful financial model, MDBs cannot do and be everything. Adopting an institutional complexity perspective at the same time highlights the power and the limits of the MDB business model. It is important to keep the findings of this study – the relevance of the financial logic and the constraints it presents to the development mandate – in mind when evaluating the development success of MDBs. When acknowledging the realities of the MDB business model, it can be employed more effectively. For instance, the volumes extended to borrowing countries can be significantly increased, without further capital increases, with the help of balance sheet optimization (Munir and Gallagher, 2020) and financial engineering such as the exposure exchange agreement between the AfDB, IBRD and IDB, and more recently the ADB (ADB, 2020b; Belhaj et al., 2017). Acknowledging the limits given by the financial logic, shareholders can consider steps to raise MDB business volumes, like twisting some financial indicators, such as slightly increasing leverage, without endangering credit ratings, accepting ratings below AAA, or stopping net income transfers to concessional and trust funds and instead letting richer shareholders pay for those causes themselves (Humphrey, 2017b, p. 19). Also, MDBs can utilize innovative financial instruments to attract financial credit, such as credit enhancement guarantees, derivatives, and innovative bond structures, all seeking to provide finance beyond what is available in markets. Similarly, the current shift from direct financing to increased private sector mobilization is a reaction to the limitations set by the financial logic in terms of capital restrictions toward significant lending expansion. Instead, mobilization seeks to leverage on MDBs' experience, networks, and favorable market access to attract additional private creditors (see, for instance, Broccolini et al., 2021).

The global role of MDBs is currently changing, away from the direct transfer of financing toward the provision of development solutions, standard setting and knowledge sharing, as well as risk mitigation, and there is an increased shift toward FCAS (Bhattacharya et al., 2018, p. 107; Prizzon et al., 2017). Nonetheless, the development and financial logics continue to be essential to MDB operations, and the two constantly interact. A thorough understanding of the interplay between the two logics and the limits they pose to each other is necessary for MDBs to fully develop their potential in tackling current global challenges and for research to fully understand MDB operations and impacts. Crucially, MDBs' success is enabled by and contingent upon their dual nature.

# Appendix

**Table A.1.** Universe of multilateral development banks

| MDB (in alphabetical order of acronym) | Founding year | Headquarters | Purpose (extract) | Portfolio structure | Shareholder structure |
|---|---|---|---|---|---|
| Asian Development Bank (ADB) | 1966 | Manila, Philippines | ". . . to foster economic growth and cooperation in the region of Asia and the Far East" | S-MDB | C-MDB |
| African Development Bank (AfDB) | 1964 | Abidjan, Côte d'Ivoire | ". . . contribute to the sustainable economic development and social progress of its regional members individually and jointly" | S-MDB | B-MDB |
| Asian Infrastructure Investment Bank (AIIB) | 2015 | Beijing, China | ". . . foster sustainable economic development, create wealth and improve infrastructure connectivity in Asia" | S-MDB | B-MDB |
| Development Bank of the Central African States (BDEAC) | 1975 | Brazzaville, Republic of Congo | ". . . to promote the economic and social development of its member states" | | B-MDB |
| West African Development Bank (BOAD) | 1973 | Lomé, Togo | ". . . to promote balance development of Member States and contribute to achieving economic integration within West Africa" | S-MDB | B-MDB |
| Black Sea Trade and Development Bank (BSTDB) | 1997 | Thessaloniki, Greece | ". . . effectively contribute to the transition process of the Member States towards the economic prosperity of the people of the region" | P-MDB | B-MDB |

| Institution | Year | Location | Mandate | | |
|---|---|---|---|---|---|
| Central American Bank for Economic Integration (CABEI) | 1960 | Tegucigalpa, Honduras | "… to promote the economic integration and the balanced economic and social development of the Central American region" | S-MDB | B-MDB |
| Development Bank of Latin American (CAF) | 1968 | Caracas, Venezuela | "… to promote sustainable development and regional integration" | S-MDB | B-MDB |
| Council of Europe Development Bank (CEDB) | 1956 | Paris, France | "… to help in solving the social problems with which European countries are or may be faced" | S-MDB | B-MDB |
| Caribbean Development Bank (CDB) | 1969 | St. Michael, Barbados | "… to finance projects and programmes contributing to the development of the region or any of the regional members" | S-MDB | B-MDB |
| East African Development Bank (EADB) | 1967 | Kampala, Uganda | "… to promote sustainable socio-economic development in East Africa" | P-MDB | B-MDB |
| European Bank for Reconstruction and Development (EBRD) | 1991 | London, United Kingdom | "… contributing to economic progress and reconstruction" and "foster the transition towards open market-oriented economies" | P-MDB | C-MDB |

**Table A.1.** (cont.)

| MDB (in alphabetical order of acronym) | Founding year | Headquarters | Purpose (extract) | Portfolio structure | Shareholder structure |
|---|---|---|---|---|---|
| Eurasian Development Bank (EDB) | 2006 | Almaty, Kazakhstan | "… to foster the strengthening and development of market economy in the member states" | P-MDB | B-MDB |
| European Investment Bank (EIB) | 1958 | Luxembourg | "… to promote European economic development and integration" | S-MDB (since 2017) | B-MDB |
| International Bank for Reconstruction and Development (IBRD) | 1944 | Washington, D.C., US | "… to assist in the reconstruction and development of territories of members" | S-MDB | C-MDB |
| Islamic Corporation for the Development of the Private Sector (ICD) | 1999 | Jeddah, Saudi Arabia | "… to complement IsDB through the development and promotion of the private sector, as a vehicle for economic growth and development in member countries" | P-MDB | B-MDB |
| International Development Agency (IDA) | 1960 (debt financed since 2018) | Washington, D.C., US | "… to promote economic development, increase productivity and thus raise standards of living in the less-developed areas of the world" | S-MDB | C-MDB |

| Name | Year | Location | Mandate | | |
|---|---|---|---|---|---|
| Inter-American Development Bank (IDB) | 1959 | Washington, D.C., US | "... to contribute to the acceleration of the process of economic and social development of the regional developing member countries, individually and collectively" | S-MDB | B-MDB |
| IDB Invest (formerly Inter-American Investment Corporation) | 1986 | Washington, D.C., US | "... to promote the economic development of its regional developing member countries" | P-MDB | B-MDB |
| International Finance Corporation (IFC) | 1956 | Washington, D.C., US | "... to further economic development by encouraging the growth of productive private enterprise in member countries" | P-MDB | C-MDB |
| International Investment Bank (IIB) | 1970 | Budapest, Hungary | "... to promote the economic development of the member states" | P-MDB | B-MDB |
| Islamic Development Bank (IsDB) | 1975 | Jeddah, Saudi Arabia | "... to foster economic development and social progress of member countries and Muslim communities individually as well as jointly in accordance with the principles of the Shari'ah" | S-MDB | B-MDB |

**Table A.1.** (cont.)

| MDB (in alphabetical order of acronym) | Founding year | Headquarters | Purpose (extract) | Portfolio structure | Shareholder structure |
|---|---|---|---|---|---|
| New Development Bank (NDB) | 2014 | Shanghai, China | "... mobilize resources for infrastructure and sustainable development projects in BRICS and other emerging economies and developing countries" | S-MDB | B-MDB |
| Nordic Investment Bank (NIB) | 1975 | Helsinki, Finland | "... to make financing available" ... "to strengthen and further develop the cooperation among [member countries]" | P-MDB | B-MDB |
| Pacific Islands Development Bank (PIDB) | 1989 | Mongmong, Guam | "... to contribute to the acceleration of the process of economic and social development of the member States and nations, individually and collectively, and to promote economic cooperation among them" | P-MDB | B-MDB |
| Trade and Development Bank (TDB), formerly PTA Bank | 1985 | *Bujumbura*, Burundi | "... to promote the economic and social development of Member States" | S-MDB | B-MDB |

**Source:** Author's own compilation based on MDB websites, charters, annual reports, and financial statements 2018; S&P Supranational Special Editions 2019, 2020. 'Purpose' is drawn from MDB charters. Some MDBs have expanded their missions beyond their initial purpose, for example to include poverty reduction.

# References

ADB (2008) *Strategy 2020: The Long-term Strategic Framework of the Asian Development Bank 2008–2020*, Manila, Asian Development Bank.

ADB (2017) *Annual Report 2017*, Manila, Asian Development Bank.

ADB (2020a) *Results Framework Indicator Definitions* [Online]. www.adb.org/sites/default/files/institutional-document/33902/rfw-indicator-definitions-apr2020.pdf (Accessed March 13, 2021).

ADB (2020b) *ADB Approves Policy Framework for Exposure Exchanges with Multilateral Development Banks*, News Release [Online]. www.adb.org/news/adb-approves-policy-framework-exposure-exchanges-multilateral-development-banks (Accessed February 3, 2021).

AfDB (2016) *Agreement Establishing the African Development Bank 2016 Edition*, Abidjan, African Development Bank.

Alacevich, M. (2008) *The World Bank's Early Reflections on Development: A Development Institution or a Bank?* World Bank, Policy Research Working Paper 4670.

Amprou, J., Guillaumont, P. and Jeanneney, S. G. (2007) "Aid selectivity according to augmented criteria," *The World Economy*, vol. 30, no. 5, pp. 733–763.

Anderson, E. and Clist, P. (2011) *Measures for Measures: Evaluating Judgements of Donor Allocative Performance*, The School of International Development, University of East Anglia, DEV Working Paper 35.

Arvanitis, Y., Stampini, M. and Vencatachellum, D. (2015) "Balancing development returns and credit risks: Project appraisal in a multilateral development bank," *Impact Assessment and Project Appraisal*, vol. 33, no. 3, pp. 195–206.

Asmild, M. (2015) "Frontier differences and the global Malmquist index," in Zhu, J. (ed.), *Data envelopment Analysis: A Handbook of Models and Methods*, Boston, Springer, pp. 447–461.

Avellán, L. and Galindo, A. (2018) *The Challenge of Countercyclicality for Multilateral Development Banks* [Online], Inter-American Development Bank. https://blogs.iadb.org/efectividad-desarrollo/en/the-challenge-of-countercyclicality-for-multilateral-development-banks/.

Babb, S. L. (2009) *Behind the Development Banks: Washington Politics, World Poverty, and the Wealth of Nations*, Chicago, University of Chicago Press.

Banker, R. D., Charnes, A. and Cooper, W. W. (1984) "Some models for estimating technical and scale inefficiencies in data envelopment analysis," *Management Science*, vol. 30, no. 9, pp. 1078–1092.

Barnett, M. N. and Coleman, L. (2005) "Designing police: Interpol and the study of change in international organizations," *International Studies Quarterly*, vol. 49, no. 4, pp. 593–620.

Barnett, M. N. and Finnemore, M. (2004) *Rules for the World: International Organizations in Global Politics*, Ithaca, N.Y., Cornell University Press.

Battilana, J., Besharov, M. and Mitzinneck, B. (2017) "On hybrids and hybrid organizing: A review and roadmap for future research," in Greenwood, R. (ed.), *The SAGE Handbook of Organizational Institutionalism*, 2nd ed., London, SAGE, pp. 128–162.

Battilana, J. and Lee, M. (2014) "Advancing research on hybrid organizing: Insights from the study of social enterprises," *The Academy of Management Annals*, vol. 8, no. 1, pp. 397–441.

Bauer, M. W. and Ege, J. (2017) "A matter of will and action: The bureaucratic autonomy of international public administrations," in Bauer, M. W., Knill, C. and Eckhard, S. (eds.), *International Bureaucracy: Challenges and Lessons for Public Administration Research*, London, Palgrave Macmillan, pp. 13–41.

Bauer, M. W., Knill, C. and Eckhard, S. (eds.) (2017) *International Bureaucracy: Challenges and Lessons for Public Administration Research*, London, Palgrave Macmillan.

Bazbauers, A. R. and Engel, S. N. (2021) *The Global Architecture of Multilateral Development Banks: A System of Debt or Development?* [Online], Abingdon, Routledge. www.taylorfrancis.com/books/978100300 7128.

Belhaj, R., Baroudi, M., Fiess, N. et al. (2017) "Exposure exchange agreements among multilateral development banks for sovereign exposures: An innovative risk management tool," *Journal of Risk Management in Financial Institutions*, vol. 10, no. 1, pp. 78–88.

Ben-Artzi, R. (2016) *Regional Development Banks in Comparison: Banking Strategies Versus Development Goals*, New York, Cambridge University Press.

Bendheim, C. L., Waddock, S. A. and Graves, S. B. (1998) "Determining best practice in corporate-stakeholder relations using data envelopment analysis," *Business & Society*, vol. 37, no. 3, pp. 306–338.

Berger, V. W. and Zhou, Y. (2005) "Kolmogorov-Smirnov tests," in Everitt, B. S. and Howell, D. C. (eds.), *Encyclopedia of Statistics in Behavioral Science*, Chichester, Wiley, pp. 1023–1026.

Bertels, S. and Lawrence, T. B. (2016) "Organizational responses to institutional complexity stemming from emerging logics: The role of individuals," *Strategic Organization*, vol. 14, no. 4, pp. 336–372.

Besharov, M. L. and Smith, W. K. (2014) 'Multiple institutional logics in organizations: Explaining their varied nature and implications," *Academy of Management Review*, vol. 39, no. 3, pp. 364–381.

Bhargava, V. (2012) "The role of the international financial institutions in addressing global issues," in Bhargava, V. (ed.), *Global Issues for Global Citizens: An Introduction to Key Development Challenges* [Online], Washington, DC, World Bank, pp. 393–409. http://hdl.handle.net/10986/7194.

Bhattacharya, A., Kharas, H., Plant, M. and Prizzon, A. (2018) "The new global agenda and the future of the multilateral development bank system," *International Organisations Research Journal*, vol. 13, no. 2, pp. 101–124.

Bikker, J. A. and Bos, J. W. B. (2008) *Bank Performance: A Theoretical and Empirical Framework for the Analysis of Profitability, Competition and Efficiency*, London, Routledge.

Birdsall, N. (2014) *The World Bank and Inter-American Development Bank: Fit for 21st Century Purpose?* Center for Global Development, CGD Policy Paper 039.

Birdsall, N. (2018) *The Dilemma of the African Development Bank: Does Governance Matter for the Long-Run Financing of the MDBs?* Center for Global Development, Working paper 498.

Birdsall, N. and Kharas, H. (2010) *Quality of Official Development Assistance Assessment*, Washington, D.C., Center for Global Development.

Birdsall, N. and Kharas, H. (2014) *The Quality of Official Development Assistance (QuODA): Third Edition*, Washington, D.C., Center for Global Development and Brookings.

Birdsall, N. and Morris, S. (2016) *Multilateral Development Banking for This Century's Development Challenges: Five Recommendations to Shareholders of the Old and New Multilateral Development Banks*, Washington, D.C., Center for Global Development.

Bourguignon, F. and Platteau, J.-P. (2017) "Does aid availability affect effectiveness in reducing poverty? A review article," *World Development*, vol. 90, pp. 6–16.

Bowman, W. (2011) *Finance Fundamentals for Nonprofits: Building Capacity and Sustainability*, Hoboken, Wiley.

Braaten, D. B. (2014) "Determinants of US foreign policy in multilateral development banks: The place of human rights," *Journal of Peace Research*, vol. 51, no. 4, pp. 515–527.

Bretton Woods Project (2017) *World Bank IDA18 to Introduce Increased Reliance on Capital Markets* [Online]. www.brettonwoodsproject.org/2017/01/world-bank-ida18-introduce-increased-reliance-capital-markets/ (Accessed March 22, 2021).

Broccolini, C., Lotti, G., Maffioli, A., Presbitero, A. F. and Stucchi, R. (2021) "Mobilization effects of multilateral development banks," *The World Bank Economic Review*, vol. 35, no. 2, pp. 521–543, https://doi.org/10.1093/wber/lhz049.

Brockett, P. L. and Golany, B. (1996) "Using rank statistics for determining programmatic efficiency differences in data envelopment analysis," *Management Science*, vol. 42, no. 3, pp. 466–472.

Brown, R. (2006) "Mismanagement or mismeasurement? Pitfalls and protocols for DEA studies in the financial services sector," *European Journal of Operational Research*, vol. 174, no. 2, pp. 1100–1116.

BSTDB (2020a) *BSTDB at a Glance* [Online], Thessaloniki, Black Sea Trade and Development Bank. www.bstdb.org/who-we-are/bstdb-at-a-glance (Accessed July 10, 2020).

BSTDB (2020b) *Investor Presentation*, Thessaloniki, Black Sea Trade and Development Bank.

Burnside, C. and Dollar, D. (2004) *Aid, Policies, and Growth: Revisiting the Evidence*, World Bank Group, World Bank Policy Research Working Paper 3251.

CEDB (2021) *Mission and History* [Online], Paris, Council of Europe Development Bank. https://coebank.org/en/about/mission/.

Charnes, A., Cooper, W. W., Lewin, A. Y. and Seiford, L. M. (eds.) (1994) *Data Envelopment Analysis: Theory, Methodology, and Applications*, Dordrecht, Springer Netherlands.

Charnes, A., Cooper, W. W. and Rhodes, E. (1978) "Measuring the efficiency of decision making units," *European Journal of Operational Research*, vol. 2, no. 6, pp. 429–444.

Cherchye, L. (2001) "Using data envelopment analysis to assess macroeconomic policy performance," *Applied Economics*, vol. 33, no. 3, pp. 407–416.

Cherchye, L., Moesen, W., Rogge, N. and van Puyenbroeck, T. (2007) "An introduction to 'benefit of the doubt' composite indicators," *Social Indicators Research*, vol. 82, no. 1, pp. 111–145.

Clifton, J., Díaz-Fuentes, D. and Gómez, A. L. (2018) "The European investment bank: Development, integration, investment?" *JCMS: Journal of Common Market Studies*, vol. 56, no. 4, pp. 733–750.

Clist, P. (2011) "25 years of aid allocation practice: Whither selectivity?" *World Development*, vol. 39, no. 10, pp. 1724–1734.

Clist, P. (2015) "Do performance measures of donors' aid allocation underperform?" *The World Economy*, vol. 38, no. 5, pp. 805–824.

Cobb, J. A., Wry, T. and Zhao, E. Y. (2016) "Funding financial inclusion: Institutional logics and the contextual contingency of funding for microfinance organizations," *Academy of Management Journal*, vol. 59, no. 6, pp. 2103–2131.

Cogneau, D. and Naudet, J.-D. (2007) "Who deserves aid? Equality of opportunity, international aid, and poverty reduction," *World Development*, vol. 35, no. 1, pp. 104–120.

Collier, P. and Dollar, D. (2002) "Aid allocation and poverty reduction," *European Economic Review*, vol. 46, no. 8, pp. 1475–1500.

Coll-Serrano, V., Bolos, V. and Suarez, R. B. (2020) *Package "deaR": Conventional and Fuzzy Data Envelopment Analysis* [Online]. https://cran .r-project.org/web/packages/deaR/deaR.pdf (Accessed January 29, 2021).

Cook, W. D., Tone, K. and Zhu, J. (2014) "Data envelopment analysis: Prior to choosing a model," *Omega*, vol. 44, pp. 1–4.

Cooper, W. W., Seiford, L. M. and Zhu, J. (2011) "Data envelopment analysis: History, models, and interpretations," in Cooper, W. W., Seiford, L. M. and Zhu, J. (eds.), *Handbook on Data Envelopment Analysis* [Online], 2nd ed., New York, Springer, pp. 1–39. http://www.springer.com/gb/BLDSS.

Delikanli, I. U., Dimitrov, T. and Agolli, R. (2018) *Multilateral Development Banks: Governance and Finance*, Basingstoke, Palgrave Macmillan.

Devinney, T. M., Yip, G. S. and Johnson, G. (2010) "Using Frontier analysis to evaluate company performance," *British Journal of Management*, vol. 21, no. 4, pp. 921–938.

DiMaggio, P. J. and Powell, W. W. (1983) "The iron cage revisited: Institutional isomorphism and collective rationality in organizational fields," *American Sociological Review*, vol. 48, no. 2, pp. 147–160.

Dollar, D. and Levin, V. (2006) "The increasing selectivity of foreign aid, 1984–2003," *World Development*, vol. 34, no. 12, pp. 2034–2046.

Dreher, A., Sturm, J.-E. and Vreeland, J. R. (2009) "Development aid and international politics: Does membership on the UN Security Council influence World Bank decisions?" *Journal of Development Economics*, vol. 88, no. 1, pp. 1–18.

Easterly, W. and Pfutze, T. (2008) "Where does the money go?: Best and worst practices in foreign aid," *Journal of Economic Perspective*, vol. 22, no. 2, pp. 29–52.

Easterly, W. and Williamson, C. R. (2011) "Rhetoric versus reality: The best and worst of aid agency practices," *World Development*, vol. 39, no. 11, pp. 1930–1949.

Ebrahim, A. and Herz, S. (2011) "The World Bank and democratic accountability: The role of civil society," in Scholte, J. A. (ed.), *Building Global Democracy?* Cambridge, Cambridge University Press, pp. 58–77.

EDB (2021) *Investors, Eurasian Development Bank* [Online]. https://eabr.org/ en/investors/ (Accessed March 13, 2021).

Edwards, S. (2018) *Can IFC Rise to Its Next Challenge?* devex.com [Online]. www.devex.com/news/can-ifc-rise-to-its-next-challenge-92746 (Accessed February 3, 2021).

Emrouznejad, A. and Yang, G. (2018) "A survey and analysis of the first 40 years of scholarly literature in DEA: 1978–2016," *Socio-Economic Planning Sciences*, vol. 61, pp. 4–8.

Faure, R., Prizzon, A. and Rogerson, A. (2015) *Multilateral Development Banks: A Short Guide*, London, Overseas Development Institute.

Fitch Ratings (2019) *Supranationals Rating Criteria: Master Criteria*, New York, Fitch Ratings.

G20 (2015) *Multilateral Development Banks: Action Plan to Optimize Balance Sheets*, Toronto, G20.

Gilbert, C. L., Powell, A. and Vines, D. (2006) "Positioning the World Bank," in Gilbert, C. L. and Vines, D. (eds.), *The World Bank: Structure and Policies*, Cambridge, Cambridge University Press, pp. 39–86.

Goodrick, E. and Reay, T. (2011) "Constellations of institutional logics," *Work and Occupations*, vol. 38, no. 3, pp. 372–416.

Greenwood, R., Raynard, M., Kodeih, F., Micelotta, E. R. and unsbury, M. (2011) "Institutional complexity and organizational responses," *The Academy of Management Annals*, vol. 5, no. 1, pp. 317–371.

Grier, W. A. (2012) *Credit Analysis of Financial Institutions*, 3rd ed., London, Euromoney Institutional Investor Plc.

Griffith-Jones, S. (2002) *Governance of the World Bank*, Paper prepared for Department for International Development.

Griffith-Jones, S. (2016) *Development Banks and their Key Roles: Supporting Investment, Structural Transformation and Sustainable Development*, Berlin, Brot für die Welt, Discussion Paper 59.

Guillaumont, P. and Wagner, L. (2015) "Performance-based allocation (PBA) of foreign aid: still alive?" in Arvin, B. M. and Lew, B. (eds.), *Handbook on the Economics of Foreign Aid*, Cheltenham, Edward Elgar, pp. 19–27.

Gutner, T. (2002) *Banking on the Environment: Multilateral Development Banks and their Environmental Performance in Central and Eastern Europe*, Cambridge, MA, MIT Press.

Gutner, T. (2005) "Explaining the gaps between mandate and performance: Agency theory and World Bank environmental reform," *Global Environmental Politics*, vol. 5, no. 2, pp. 10–37.

Gutner, T. (2017) *International Organizations in World Politics*, Thousand Oaks, SAGE/CQ Press.

Gutner, T. and Thompson, A. (2010) "The politics of IO performance: A framework," *The Review of International Organizations*, vol. 5, no. 3, pp. 227–248.

Hassan, M. K. and Lewis, M. K. (2007) "Islamic banking: An introduction and overview," in Hassan, M. K. and Lewis, M. K. (eds.), *Handbook of Islamic Banking* [Online], Cheltenham, Elgar, pp. 1–17. http://site.ebrary.com/lib/alltitles/docDetail.action?docID=10328592.

Hawkins, D. G., Lake, D. A., Nielson, D. L. and Tierney, M. J. (eds.) (2006a) *Delegation and Agency in International Organizations*, Cambridge, Cambridge University Press.

Hawkins, D. G., Lake, D. A., Nielson, D. L. and Tierney, M. J. (2006b) "Delegation under anarchy: States, international organizations, and principal-agent theory," in Hawkins, D. G., Lake, D. A., Nielson, D. L. and Tierney, M. J. (eds.), *Delegation and Agency in International Organizations*, Cambridge, Cambridge University Press, pp. 3–38.

Heldt, E. C. and Schmidtke, H. (2019) "Explaining coherence in international regime complexes: How the World Bank shapes the field of multilateral development finance," *Review of International Political Economy*, vol. 26, no. 6, pp. 1160–1186.

Huguenin, J.-M. (2012) *Data Envelopment Analysis (DEA): A Pedagogical Guide for Decision Makers in the Public Sector*, Lausanne, IDHEAP.

Humphrey, C. (2014) "The politics of loan pricing in multilateral development banks," *Review of International Political Economy*, vol. 21, no. 3, pp. 611–639.

Humphrey, C. (2016a) "The 'hassle factor' of MDB lending and borrower demand in Latin America," in Park, S. and Strand, J. R. (eds.), *Global Economic Governance and the Development Practices of the Multilateral Development Banks*, Abingdon, Routledge, pp. 143–166.

Humphrey, C. (2016b) "The invisible hand: Financial pressures and organisational convergence in multilateral development banks," *The Journal of Development Studies*, vol. 52, no. 1, pp. 92–112.

Humphrey, C. (2017a) "He who pays the piper calls the tune: Credit rating agencies and multilateral development banks," *The Review of International Organizations*, vol. 12, no. 2, pp. 281–306.

Humphrey, C. (2017b) "Maximising the financial potential of the multilateral development banks – without a capital increase," in *Six Recommendations for Reforming Multilateral Development Banks – An Essay Series*, London, Overseas Development Institute, pp. 17–20.

Humphrey, C. (2019) "Minilateral' development banks: What the rise of Africa's trade and development bank says about multilateral governance," *Development and Change*, vol. 50, no. 1, pp. 164–190.

Humphrey, C. and Michaelowa, K. (2013) "Shopping for development: Multilateral lending, shareholder composition and borrower preferences," *World Development*, vol. 44, pp. 142–155.

Hurd, I. (1999) "Legitimacy and authority in international politics," *International Organization*, vol. 53, no. 2, pp. 379–408.

IBRD (2020) *Who We Are* [Online], International Bank for Reconstruction and Development. www.worldbank.org/en/who-we-are/ibrd (Accessed July 10, 2020).

IDB (2021) *Investors: Home*, Inter-American Development [Online]. www .iadb.org/en/investors/investors (Accessed March 13, 2021).

IFC (n.d.) *How IFC Measures the Development Impact of Its Interventions*, International Finance Corporation [Online]. www.ifc.org/wps/wcm/connect/af1377f3-4792-4bb0-ba83-a0664dda0e55/202012-IFC-AIMM-brochure.pdf? MOD=AJPERES&CVID=noLTBSi (Accessed January 3, 2021).

IFC (2021) *About IFC: Investor Relations*, International Finance Corporation [Online]. www.ifc.org/wps/wcm/connect/CORP_EXT_Content/IFC_ External_Corporate_Site/About+IFC_New/Investor+Relations/ (Accessed March 13, 2021).

IIB (2021) *General Information*, International Investment Bank [Online]. https://iib.int/en/about (Accessed March 13, 2021).

Institute of Development Studies (2000) *A Foresight and Policy Study of the Multilateral Development Banks*, Development Financing Study 2000:2, Stockholm:.

IsDB (2013) *Islamic Development Bank Group in Brief*, Jeddah, Islamic Development Bank Group.

Jomo, K. S. and Chowdhury, A. (2019) "World Bank Financializing Development," *Development*, vol. 62, 1–4, pp. 147–153.

Kapoor, S. (2019) *Billions to Trillions: A Reality Check*, RE-DEFINE, Policy Brief for Stamp Out Poverty, London .

Kapur, D., Lewis, J. P. and Webb, R. C. (eds.) (1997) *The World Bank: Its First Half Century*, Washington, DC, Brookings Institution Press.

Kapur, D. and Raychaudhuri, A. (2014) *Rethinking the Financial Design of the World Bank*, Washington, D.C., Center for Global Development, Working Paper 352.

Karagiannis, R. and Karagiannis, G. (2018) "Intra- and inter-group composite indicators using the BoD model," *Socio-Economic Planning Sciences*, vol. 61, pp. 44–51.

Kaufmann, D., Kraay, A. and Mastruzzi, M. (2011) "The worldwide governance indicators: Methodology and analytical issues," *Hague Journal on the Rule of Law*, vol. 3, no. 02, pp. 220–246.

Kellerman, M. (2019) "The proliferation of multilateral development banks," *The Review of International Organizations*, vol. 14, pp. 107–145.

Kenny, C., Morris, S. and Ramachandran, V. (2018) *Does the IFC Capital Increase Add Up?*, Center for Global Development, Commentary & Analysis [Online]. www.cgdev.org/blog/does-ifc-capital-increase-add (Accessed February 3, 2021).

Kersting, E. and Kilby, C. (2021) "Do domestic politics shape U.S. influence in the World Bank?" *The Review of International Organizations,* vol. 16, no.1, pp. 29–58.

Kharas, H. and Noe, L. (2018) *How should Official Development Assistance be Allocated across Countries?: A Market Test for Aid Allocation and Country Graduation*, Brookings, Global Economy & Development Working Paper 125.

Kilby, C. (2006) "Donor influence in multilateral development banks: The case of the Asian Development Bank," *The Review of International Organizations*, vol. 1, no. 2, pp. 173–195.

Knack, S., Rogers, F. H. and Eubank, N. (2011) "Aid quality and donor rankings," *World Development*, vol. 39, no. 11, pp. 1907–1917.

Kodera, K. (2017) *How should the Multilateral Development Banks Stay Relevant in the Sustainable Development Goal Era?* London, Overseas Development Institute.

Kraatz, M. S. and Block, E. S. (2008) "Organizational implications of institutional pluralism," in Greenwood, R. (ed.), *The Sage Handbook of Organizational Institutionalism*, Los Angeles [u.a.], SAGE, pp. 243–275.

Krasner, S. D. (ed.) (1983) *International Regimes*, Ithaca, Cornell University Press.

Kuosmanen, T. (2009) "Data envelopment analysis with missing data," *Journal of the Operational Research Society*, vol. 60, no. 12, pp. 1767–1774.

Lebovics, M., Hermes, N. and Hudon, M. (2016) "Are financial and social efficiency mutually exclusive?: A case study of vietnamese microfinance institutions," *Annals of Public and Cooperative Economics*, vol. 87, no. 1, pp. 55–77.

Lee, C.-F. and Lee, A. C. (2013) "Terms and essays," in Lee, C.-F. and Lee, A. C. (eds.), *Encyclopedia of Finance*, Boston, Springer, pp. 3–204.

Liu, J. S., Lu, L. Y. and Lu, W.-M. (2016) "Research fronts in data envelopment analysis," *Omega*, vol. 58, pp. 33–45.

Lovell, C. A. K. and Pastor, J. T. (1999) "Radial DEA models without inputs or without outputs," *European Journal of Operational Research*, vol. 118, no. 1, pp. 46–51.

Lyne, M. M., Nielson, D. L. and Tierney, M. J. (2006) "Who delegates?: Alternative models of principals in development aid," in Hawkins, D. G.,

Lake, D. A., Nielson, D. L. and Tierney, M. J. (eds.), *Delegation and Agency in International Organizations*, Cambridge, Cambridge University Press, pp. 41–76.

Lyne, M. M., Nielson, D. L. and Tierney, M. J. (2009) "Controlling coalitions: Social lending at the multilateral development banks," *The Review of International Organizations*, vol. 4, no. 4, pp. 407–433.

Mair, J., Mayer, J. and Lutz, E. (2015) "Navigating institutional plurality: Organizational governance in hybrid organizations," *Organization Studies*, vol. 36, no. 6, pp. 713–739.

McGillivray, M. (1989) "The allocation of aid among developing countries: A multi-donor analysis using a per capita aid index," *World Development*, vol. 17, no. 4, pp. 561–568.

McGillivray, M. (2004) "Descriptive and prescriptive analyses of aid allocation: Approaches, issues, and consequences," *International Review of Economics & Finance*, vol. 13, no. 3, pp. 275–292.

McGillivray, M. and Clarke, M. (2018) "Fairness in the international allocation of development aid," *The World Economy*, vol. 41, no. 4, pp. 1068–1087.

Mistry, P. S. (1995) *Multilateral Development Banks: An Assessment of their Financial Structures, Policies and Practices*, The Hague, FONDAD.

Mohammed, A. A. (2004) *Who Pays for the World Bank?*, G-24, Research Papers.

Moody's (2017) *Multilateral Development Banks and Other Supranational Entities: Rating Methodology*, New York, Moody's.

Moody's (2019) *Multilateral Development Banks and Other Supranational Entities: Rating Methodology*, New York, Moody's.

Munir, W. and Gallagher, K. P. (2020) "Scaling up for sustainable development: Benefits and costs of expanding and optimizing balance sheet in the multilateral development banks," *Journal of International Development*, vol. 32, no. 2, pp. 222–243.

Murphy, G. B., Trailer, J. W. and Hill, R. C. (1996) "Measuring performance in entrepreneurship research," *Journal of Business Research*, vol. 36, no. 1, pp. 15–23.

Nielson, D. L. and Tierney, M. J. (2003) "Delegation to international organizations: Agency theory and World Bank environmental reform," *International Organization*, vol. 57, no. 2, pp. 241–276.

O'Donnell, C. J., Rao, D. S. P. and Battese, G. E. (2008) "Metafrontier frameworks for the study of firm-level efficiencies and technology ratios," *Empirical Economics*, vol. 34, no. 2, pp. 231–255.

Ocasio, W. and Gai, S. L. (2020) "Institutions: Everywhere but not everything," *Journal of Management Inquiry*, vol. 29, no. 3, pp. 262–271.

Ocasio, W. and Radoynovska, N. (2016) "Strategy and commitments to institutional logics: Organizational heterogeneity in business models and governance," *Strategic Organization*, vol. 14, no. 4, pp. 287–309.

Ocasio, W., Thornton, P. H. and Lounsbury, M. (2017) "Advances to the institutional logics perspective," in Greenwood, R. (ed.), *The SAGE Handbook of Organizational Institutionalism*, 2nd ed., London, SAGE, pp. 509–531.

OECD (2021) OECD.Stat (database) [Online]. https://stats.oecd.org/Index.aspx?DataSetCode=MULTISYSTEM.

Oestreich, J. E. (ed.) (2012) *International Organizations as Self-directed Actors: A Framework for Analysis*, London, Routledge.

Oliver, C. (1991) "Strategic responses to institutional processes," *Academy of Management Review*, vol. 16, no. 1, p. 145.

Pache, A.-C. and Santos, F. (2010) "When worlds collide: The internal dynamics of organizational responses to conflicting institutional demands," *Academy of Management Review*, vol. 35, no. 3, pp. 455–476.

Pache, A.-C. and Santos, F. (2013) 'Inside the hybrid organization: Selective coupling as a response to competing institutional logics," *Academy of Management Journal*, vol. 56, no. 4, pp. 972–1001.

Park, S. (2010) *World Bank Group Interactions with Environmentalists: Changing International Organisation Identities*, Manchester, Manchester University Press.

Park, S. and Strand, J. R. (2016) "Global economic governance and the development practices of the multilateral development banks," in Park, S. and Strand, J. R. (eds.), *Global Economic Governance and the Development Practices of the Multilateral Development Banks*, Abingdon, Routledge, pp. 3–20.

Park, S. and Weaver, C. (2012) "The anatomy of autonomy: The case of the World Bank," in Oestreich, J. E. (ed.), *International Organizations as Self-directed Actors: A Framework for Analysis*, London, Routledge, pp. 91–117.

Peitz, L. (2022) *Multilateral Development Banks: Mission, Business Model, Financial Management*, Hertie School, Research Repository Publications.

Pfeffer, J. and Salancik, G. R. (1978) *The External Control of Organizations: A Resource Dependence Perspective*, New York, Harper & Row.

Pietschmann, E. (2014) *Forgotten or Unpromising? The Elusive Phenomenon of Under-aided Countries, Sectors and Sub-national Regions*, Bonn, Deutsches Institut fur Entwicklungspolitik.

Prentice, C. R. (2016) "Why so many measures of nonprofit financial performance? Analyzing and improving the use of financial measures in nonprofit research," *Nonprofit and Voluntary Sector Quarterly*, vol. 45, no. 4, pp. 715–740.

Prior, D. and Surroca, J. (2006) "Strategic groups based on marginal rates: An application to the Spanish banking industry," *European Journal of Operational Research*, vol. 170, no. 1, pp. 293–314.

Prizzon, A., Humphrey, C., Kaul, I. et al. (2017) *Six Recommendations for Reforming Multilateral Development Banks: An Essay Series*, London, Overseas Development Institute.

Rabar, D. (2017) "An overview of data envelopment analysis application in studies on the socio-economic performance of OECD countries," *Economic Research-Ekonomska Istraživanja*, vol. 30, no. 1, pp. 1770–1784.

Rauh, C. and Zürn, M. (2020) "Authority, politicization, and alternative justifications: endogenous legitimation dynamics in global economic governance 1," *Review of International Political Economy*, vol. 27, no. 3, pp. 583–611.

Ray, R. (2019) *Who Controls Multilateral Development Finance?* Global Economic Governance Initiative, GEGI Working Paper 026.

Ray, R. and Kamal, R. (2019) "Can south–south cooperation compete? The development bank of Latin America and the Islamic development bank," *Development and Change*, vol. 50, no. 1, pp. 191–220.

Raynard, M. (2016) "Deconstructing complexity: Configurations of institutional complexity and structural hybridity," *Strategic Organization*, vol. 14, no. 4, pp. 310–335.

Reay, T. and Hinings, C. R. (2009) "Managing the rivalry of competing institutional logics," *Organization Studies*, vol. 30, no. 6, pp. 629–652.

Reay, T. and Jones, C. (2016) "Qualitatively capturing institutional logics," *Strategic Organization*, vol. 14, no. 4, pp. 441–454.

Reichert, P. (2018) "A meta-analysis examining the nature of trade-offs in microfinance," *Oxford Development Studies*, vol. 46, no. 3, pp. 430–452.

Rich, B. (2013) *Foreclosing the Future: The World Bank and the Politics of Environmental Destruction*, Washington, DC, Island Press/Center for Resource Economics; Imprint: Island Press.

Roodman, D. (2012) *An Index of Donor Performance*, Center for Global Development, Working Paper 67.

Ryan, C. and Irvine, H. (2012) "Not-for-profit ratios for financial resilience and internal accountability: A study of Australian international aid organisations," *Australian Accounting Review*, vol. 22, no. 2, pp. 177–194.

S&P (2015) *Supranationals Special Edition 2015*, New York, Standard & Poor's.

S&P (2016) *Supranationals Special Edition 2016*, New York, Standard & Poor's.

S&P (2018) *Supranationals Special Edition 2018*, New York, Standard & Poor's.

S&P (2019) *Supranationals Special Edition 2019*, New York, Standard & Poor's.

S&P (2020) *Supranationals Special Edition 2020*, New York, Standard & Poor's.

Sagasti, F. R. and Prada, F. (2006) "Regional development banks: A comparative perspective," in Ocampo, J. A. (ed.), *Regional Financial Cooperation* [Online], Washington, DC, Santiago, Chile?, Brookings Institution Press; United Nations Economic Commission for Latin America and the Caribbean, pp. 68–106. www.jstor.org/stable/10.7864/j.ctt127w7z.

Sarkis, J. (2007) "Preparing your data for DEA," in Zhu, J. and Cook, W. D. (eds.), *Modeling Data Irregularities and Structural Complexities in Data Envelopment Analysis*, New York, Springer, pp. 305–320.

Scheel, H. (2001) "Undesirable outputs in efficiency valuations," *European Journal of Operational Research*, vol. 132, no. 2, pp. 400–410.

Schettler, L. V. (2020) *Socializing Development: Transnational Social Movement Advocacy and the Human Rights Accountability of Multilateral Development Banks*, Bielefeld, Transcript Verlag.

Schneider, C. and Tobin, J. (2011) *Eenie, Meenie, Miney, Moe?: Institutional Portfolios and Delegation to Multilateral Aid Institutions*, Working paper, 10.2139/ssrn.1949238.

Simar, L. and Wilson, P. W. (1998) "Sensitivity analysis of efficiency scores: How to bootstrap in nonparametric Frontier models," *Management Science*, vol. 44, no. 1, pp. 49–61.

Simar, L. and Wilson, P. W. (2011) "Performance of the bootstrap for DEA estimators and iterating the principle," in Cooper, W. W., Seiford, L. M. and Zhu, J. (eds.), *Handbook on Data Envelopment Analysis* [Online], 2nd ed., New York, Springer, pp. 241–271. www.springer.com/gb/BLDSS.

Sobol, M. (2016) "Principal-agent analysis and pathological delegation: The (almost) untold story," *Governance*, vol. 29, no. 3, pp. 335–350.

Staessens, M., Kerstens, P. J., Bruneel, J. and Cherchye, L. (2019) "Data envelopment analysis and social enterprises: Analysing performance, strategic orientation and mission drift," *Journal of Business Ethics*, vol. 159, pp. 325–341.

Stein, F. and Sridhar, D. (2017) *The World Bank Reinvents Itself – and Puts Poverty Reduction at Risk* [Online]. https://theconversation.com/the-world-bank-reinvents-itself-and-puts-poverty-reduction-at-risk-79403 (Accessed March 22, 2021).

Sueyoshi, T. and Yuan, Y. (2016) "Marginal rate of transformation and rate of substitution measured by DEA environmental assessment: Comparison among European and North American nations," *Energy Economics*, vol. 56, pp. 270–287.

Tallberg, J. and Zürn, M. (2019) "The legitimacy and legitimation of international organizations: Introduction and framework," *The Review of International Organizations*, vol. 14, no. 4, pp. 581–606.

Thorne, J. and Du Toit, C. (2009) "A macro-framework for successful development banks," *Development Southern Africa*, vol. 26, no. 5, pp. 677–694.

Thornton, P. H. and Ocasio, W. (1999) "Institutional logics and the historical contingency of power in organizations: Executive succession in the higher education publishing industry, 1958–1990," *American Journal of Sociology*, vol. 105, no. 3, pp. 801–843.

Thornton, P. H., Ocasio, W. and Lounsbury, M. (2012) *The Institutional Logics Perspective: A New Approach to Culture, Structure and Process*, Oxford, Oxford University Press.

Thornton, P. H., Ocasio, W. and Lounsbury, M. (2015) "The institutional logics perspective," in Scott, R. A. and Kosslyn, S. M. (eds.), *Emerging Trends in the Social and Behavioral Sciences*, Hoboken, NJ, Wiley, pp. 1–22.

Tierney, M. J., Nielson, D. L., Hawkins, D. G. et al. (2011) "More dollars than sense: Refining our knowledge of development finance using aiddata," *World Development*, vol. 39, no. 11, pp. 1891–1906.

van Puyenbroeck, T. and Rogge, N. (2020) "Comparing regional human development using global frontier difference indices," *Socio-Economic Planning Sciences*, vol. 70, pp. 1–8.

Vázquez, S. T. (2015) "Geographical allocation of aid: Lessons from political economy," in Arvin, B. M. and Lew, B. (eds.), *Handbook on the Economics of Foreign Aid*, Cheltenham, Edward Elgar, pp. 90–108.

Vermeulen, P. A., Zietsma, C., Greenwood, R. and Langley, A. (2016) "Strategic responses to institutional complexity," *Strategic Organization*, vol. 14, no. 4, pp. 277–286.

Vestergaard, J. and Wade, R. H. (2013) "Protecting power: How Western states retain the dominant voice in the World Bank's governance," *World Development*, vol. 46, pp. 153–164.

Wade, R. H. (2002) "US hegemony and the World Bank: the fight over people and ideas," *Review of International Political Economy*, vol. 9, no. 2, pp. 201–229.

Walheer, B. (2018) "Aggregation of metafrontier technology gap ratios: the case of European sectors in 1995-2015," *European Journal of Operational Research*, vol. 269, no. 3, pp. 1013–1026.

Weaver, C. (2008) *Hypocrisy Trap: The World Bank and the Poverty of Reform*, Princeton, Princeton University Press.

Weisbrod, B. A. (1998a) "The nonprofit mission and its financing: Growing links between nonprofits and the rest of the economy," in Weisbrod, B. A.

(ed.), *To Profit or not to Profit: The Commercial Transformation of the Nonprofit Sector*, Cambridge, Cambridge University Press, pp. 1–22.

Weisbrod, B. A. (ed.) (1998b) *To Profit or not to Profit: The Commercial Transformation of the Nonprofit Sector*, Cambridge, Cambridge University Press.

White, H. and McGillivray, M. (1995) "How well is aid allocated? Descriptive measures of aid allocation: A survey of methodology and results," *Development and Change*, vol. 26, no. 1, pp. 163–183.

Wood, A. (2008) "Looking ahead optimally in allocating aid," *World Development*, vol. 36, no. 7, pp. 1135–1151.

Woods, N. (2006) *The Globalizers: The IMF, the World Bank, and Their Borrowers*, Ithaca, Cornell University Press.

World Bank (2018) *IDA Makes Historic Capital Market Debut with Inaugural US$1.5 Billion Benchmark Bond: First IDA bond nearly five times oversubscribed*, Press release [Online]. www.worldbank.org/en/news/press-release/2018/04/17/ida-makes-historic-capital-market-debut-with-inaugural-usd-1-5-billion-benchmark-bond (Accessed February 26, 2021).

World Bank (2019a) *World Development Indicators* [Online]. https://databank.worldbank.org/reports.aspx?source=world-development-indicators.

World Bank (2019b) *Worldwide Governance Indicators* [Online]. https://databank.worldbank.org/reports.aspx?source=worldwide-governance-indicators.

World Bank and OECD (2021) *AidFlows* [Online]. www.aidflows.org/ (Accessed September 1, 2021).

World Bank Group (2020) *Results and Performance of the World Bank Group 2020: An Independent Evaluation*. Washington, D.C., World Bank Group.

Wry, T., Cobb, J. A. and Aldrich, H. E. (2013) "More than a metaphor: Assessing the historical legacy of resource dependence and its contemporary promise as a theory of environmental complexity," *The Academy of Management Annals*, vol. 7, no. 1, pp. 441–488.

Zetter, R. (2021) "Theorizing the refugee humanitarian-development nexus: A political-economy analysis," *Journal of Refugee Studies*, vol. 34, no. 2, pp. 1766–1786.

Zhao, E. Y. and Lounsbury, M. (2016) "An institutional logics approach to social entrepreneurship: Market logic, religious diversity, and resource acquisition by microfinance organizations," *Journal of Business Venturing*, vol. 31, no. 6, pp. 643–662.

# Acknowledgments

I am grateful to Tamar Gutner, Johanna Mair, and the late Henrik Enderlein for their continuous support and valuable feedback on this work; to my interview partners for sharing their expertise; to the German Academic Scholarship Foundation, the Fritz Thyssen Foundation, the Hertie School and the Berlin Graduate School for Global and Transregional Studies for funding research and writing.

# Cambridge Elements ≡

# International Relations

## Series Editors

### Jon C. W. Pevehouse
*University of Wisconsin–Madison*

Jon C. W. Pevehouse is the Vilas Distinguished Achievement Professor of Political Science at the University of Wisconsin–Madison. He has published numerous books and articles in IR in the fields of international political economy, international organizations, foreign policy analysis, and political methodology. He is a former editor of the leading IR field journal, International Organization.

### Tanja A. Börzel
*Freie Universität Berlin*

Tanja A. Börzel is the Professor of political science and holds the Chair for European Integration at the Otto-Suhr-Institute for Political Science, Freie Universität Berlin. She holds a PhD from the European University Institute, Florence, Italy. She is coordinator of the Research College "The Transformative Power of Europe," as well as the FP7-Collaborative Project "Maximizing the Enlargement Capacity of the European Union" and the H2020 Collaborative Project "The EU and Eastern Partnership Countries: An Inside-Out Analysis and Strategic Assessment." She directs the Jean Monnet Center of Excellence "Europe and its Citizens."

### Edward D. Mansfield
*University of Pennsylvania*

Edward D. Mansfield is the Hum Rosen Professor of Political Science, University of Pennsylvania. He has published well over 100 books and articles in the area of international political economy, international security, and international organizations. He is Director of the Christopher H. Browne Center for International Politics at the University of Pennsylvania and former program co-chair of the American Political Science Association.

## Editorial Team

**International Relations Theory**
Jeffrey T. Checkel, European University Institute, Florence
Miles Kahler, American University Washington, D.C.

**International Security**
Sarah Kreps, Cornell University
Anna Leander, Graduate Institute Geneva

**International Political Economy**
Edward D. Mansfield, University of Pennsylvania
Stafanie Walter, University of Zurich

**International Organisations**
Tanja A. Börzel, Freie Universität Berlin
Jon C. W. Pevehouse, University of Wisconsin–Madison

## About the Series

The Cambridge Elements Series in International Relations publishes original research on key topics in the field. The series includes manuscripts addressing international security, international political economy, international organizations, and international relations.

Cambridge Elements ≡

# International Relations

## Elements in the Series

Printed in the United States
by Baker & Taylor Publisher Services